GAY

—— *and* ——

Catholic

"By turns hilarious, thoughtful, constructive, and searingly honest, *Gay and Catholic* is a must-read for anyone who believes the terms are mutually exclusive, for anyone who thinks seriously about Catholicism and the pastoral care of the homosexual person, for anyone who thinks they've already figured it all out. Eve Tushnet has written a humane, brave, and groundbreaking book that demolishes assumptions. If you think you know what she is going to say, you don't. So you need to read this."

Elizabeth Scalia
Author of *Strange Gods: Unmasking the Idols in Everyday Life*

"I know that some people somewhere may consider this a controversial book, but it is hard for me to think of anything so kind, honest, non-doctrinaire, commonsensical, and good-humored as controversial. [My situation as husband, father, and grandfather is obviously quite different than the author's, but] as a Catholic I found material for self-reflection on virtually every page. This book was a real grace for me, as it will no doubt be for many others trying to live as disciples of Jesus."

Peter Steinfels
Codirector of the Center on Religion and Culture
Fordham University

"I recommend Eve Tushnet's new book, not because I agree with everything in it—I don't—but because I learned a lot from it. I believe others will learn from it, too. Unlike just about everyone else who writes on issues of sexuality, morality, and marriage, Eve is impossible to classify. She's a devout Catholic, but scarcely qualifies as a 'conservative.' She self-identifies as 'gay,' but most others who identify themselves in that way will not find themselves sympathizing with her ideas and arguments. Still, few have thought as deeply or as creatively as has she about same-sex attraction and its existential significance for persons who experience it. Readers across the spectrum will be informed and challenged by her reflections."

Robert P. George
McCormick Professor of Jurisprudence
Princeton University

"Eve Tushnet's conversion story and subsequent gradual surrender to the faith make for a fascinating read—full of wry humor, practical advice, humility, and best of all, deliciously pungent word craft. Full of insight, there is plenty to chew on in *Gay and Catholic*, which is part memoir, part guidebook, and honest to the core."

Simcha Fisher
Author of *The Sinner's Guide to Natural Family Planning*

"Eve Tushnet puts a human face on Church teaching. With unassuming but total candor, she describes her experience of the challenge and joy of living as an openly lesbian woman who is deeply attached to her Catholic faith. Her account will open a new window on human and Christian experience for many people inside and outside the Church."

Rev. Louis J. Cameli
Author of *Catholic Teaching on Homosexuality*

"Honest, fresh, and tremendously helpful, Eve Tushnet's new book offers a roadmap for Catholics experiencing same-sex attraction. Using her own experiences as a gay, celibate Catholic convert, Eve shows how the celibate vocation offers both a cross and a crown. For a firsthand look at this challenging but grace-filled path, as well as practical tips for helping same-sex attracted friends and family, read this book."

Brandon Vogt
Author of *Saints and Social Justice*

"Eve Tushnet has written a book that's hard to read and that challenges every assumption you might have never known you had. Open your mind and bare your heart with her, because what you have in your hands might just be the most important book of our age. It's raw and honest and critical, with some laughter and tears on top. Truly a book that's not just a keeper, but a sharer, too."

Sarah Reinhard
Blogger at *Snoring Scholar*

GAY

— *and* —

Catholic

Accepting My Sexuality, Finding Community, Living My Faith

Eve Tushnet

Ave Maria Press AVE Notre Dame, Indiana

The poem "Don't Surrender" is from the Penguin publication *The Gift: Collected Poems of Hafiz*, by Daniel Ladinsky. Copyright © 1999 Daniel Ladinsky and used with his permission.

Founded in 1865, Ave Maria Press is a ministry of the United States Province of Holy Cross.

www.avemariapress.com

Paperback: ISBN-13 978-1-59471-542-6

E-book: ISBN-13 978-1-59471-543-3

Cover and text design by Andy Wagoner.

Printed and bound in the United States of America.

Library of Congress Cataloging-in-Publication Data

Tushnet, Eve.

  Gay and Catholic : accepting my sexuality, finding community, living my faith / Eve Tushnet.

       pages cm

  Includes bibliographical references.

  ISBN 978-1-59471-542-6 (pbk.) -- ISBN 978-1-59471-543-3 (ebook)

  1. Lesbians--Religious life. 2. Catholic gays--Religious life. 3. Homosexuality--Religious aspects--Catholic Church. I. Title.

  BX2373.L46T87 2014

  282.086'64--dc23

                                            2014012303

Contents

Introduction

"But I'm not a saint yet. I'm an alcoholic. I'm a drug addict. I'm homosexual. I'm a genius. Of course, I could be all four of these dubious things and still be a saint."

—Truman Capote, *Music for Chameleons*

I was born in 1978, came out of the closet at age thirteen or so, and was received into the Catholic Church during my sophomore year of college.

When I became Catholic in 1998, I didn't know any other gay, lesbian, or bisexual people who intended to be faithful to the Church's teachings on sexuality. I didn't even know *of* any such people. As far as I could tell, I was completely unprecedented. Nonetheless, I had all the humility of your average sophomore-year convert, so I didn't worry about how I'd manage without any forerunners or guides.

Since that time I've learned that many other people have walked this road before me. I've discovered the Church's hidden treasures of history, theology, art, and saints' lives, which have taught me that a faithful, chaste gay life can be beautiful and fruitful. In this book I share what I and others have discovered: that being gay and faithful to the historical Christian teaching on sexuality need *not* condemn you to a life of barren loneliness. I'm honest about the sufferings and humiliations inherent in this way of life—every vocation has its own forms of loneliness, its own typical crosses—but I focus on the forms of love that are available to you. Every person has a unique call from God to love and serve others and to receive their love. This is what Catholics often call a person's *vocation*. Vocations go beyond obvious ones such as marriage or the priesthood; I explore the vocations, the paths of

1

love, that are open to people who are not called to marriage or to vowed religious life.

This book is not "about" the Catholic or historical Christian teaching on homosexuality. This is not a book about why people are gay or why the Catholic Church teaches what it teaches. I take the Church's position on homosexuality more or less for granted here, although I point you toward resources if you do want to explore the theology (see appendix one).

But this also isn't solely a personal story. This is a book about what God might want *you* to do with your love and your life if you are attracted to and fall in love with members of your own sex—not about what you shouldn't do or why you shouldn't do it. It's not just about what I personally do, although I give you my own story and suggest lessons I've drawn from it. But this is a book I hope will help people in many different situations discern how God is calling them.

God wants you to love. He wants you to increase the tenderness and beauty in his world. This book is about the many different ways in which that call to love can play out for people who are gay or experience same-sex attraction *and* accept the historical Christian teaching on chastity.

Here's where I'm coming from and how this book differs from many of the other books on this topic:

I'm a woman. Most of the people who have written about being gay and celibate for religious reasons have been men. In any question of sexuality, it's important to hear from both sexes; and it's especially important that women's voices be a part of the conversation about sexual orientation, in which the stereotypes applied to gay men are so different from those applied to lesbians.

I'm in no sense ex-gay. In fact, I seem to become more lesbian with time—college was my big fling with bisexuality, my passing phase. I don't think marriage is part of my vocation, so I've had to explore other paths. Most of this book is about those paths.

I had a good childhood, a gay-supportive family, and truly fruitful experiences within gay communities. For these reasons, what I have to say may not speak as much to people who experienced more childhood pain, who feared or experienced familial rejection, or who found gay communities unwelcoming or shallow. I realize that especially when it comes to my family's acceptance I may be in the minority (although I hope that's changing), and I hope I express gratitude for that throughout the book rather than taking it for granted. But a lot of the books and other writings directed toward gay Christians describe types of psychological pain I don't think I've experienced and that other gay Christians may also have been able to avoid. And—more problematically—these books tend to assume that gay communities are like fairy gold, which looks like real gold but turns to dead leaves overnight. So, too, gay communities are presented as attractive and perhaps even liberating at first, but ultimately hollow and worthless. There needs to be a book directed at people who still find beauty, mutual aid, and solidarity in gay life, even though we believe we've found something much greater in Christ.

Chastity and sexual orientation issues haven't been my most difficult ongoing struggles as a Catholic. I'd say alcoholism has probably been the toughest one. I want to write a book that is honest about how you can find your deepest joy and solace in the Church, yet still remain imprisoned by addiction. I want to get past the clichés on both sides: the sad, angry, and man-hating lesbian drinking away the pain of her sexual brokenness or the miserable, life-denying celibate who has been twisted by the evil Catholic Church. While this book does not focus on recovery, I hope it's honest when addiction and recovery are discussed.

In every gay celibate life, the crosses (and joys) of celibacy will inevitably be accompanied by other struggles, other challenges, other temptations, and other losses. I offer some ideas about how the tools we use in developing chaste, celibate vocations within the Church can also arm us against other demons we may need to fight.

There's a certain catch-22 in writing about celibate gay life. If you write about the joy you find in fidelity to Christ and the Church, you may sound Pollyannaish, defensive, or callous toward others' suffering. If you write about the difficulties, you can be accused of self-pity and masochism. I hope that this book is honest about the suffering that comes with this form of life in Christ but is also quick to note the joys it can bring.

This book is *not* a theological treatise defending the Catholic Church's teaching on sexuality. I admittedly don't always understand that teaching, and I don't think you need to understand every single element of a Church teaching in order to assent to its authority in your life. And you certainly don't need to accept any one school of theology—such as natural law—in order to accept and live by the Catholic ideal of chastity. If you do want to explore the reasoning and scriptural interpretation that shape the Church's teaching, I've included some reading recommendations in appendix one, but you really don't have to spend a lot of time on this stuff if you don't want to.

This is also not a book about politics. Gay and same-sex attracted Christians may disagree among ourselves on the best resolutions to the many heated political debates surrounding gay rights; this book is about the lives we can make for ourselves, in response to God's call, regardless of our political opinions.

When I first entered the Catholic Church I thought of my role—a lesbian-gay-bisexual-queer-same-sex-attracted Christian—as having two parts: the negative act of not having gay sex and the positive act of intellectually understanding the Church's teachings. I now see my task much more simply, as the discernment and living out of my vocations: figuring out how God is calling me to love and then pouring myself out into that love.

Part one of this book is mostly autobiographical. I give you a sense of where I'm coming from, how I first encountered Catholicism and what I thought of it, how I ultimately found myself saying yes to the Church, and what happened in the long years after my Baptism and Confirmation. I also offer a more theoretical discussion of "origin stories" for homosexuality. Does it matter why you're gay? Should it matter to Christians? I argue that there are many different kinds of homosexuality, some of which may have psychological origin stories and some of which don't, and also that the contemporary American Christian focus on the psychological past has distracted us from the far more important subject of the vocational future. And I emphasize the diversity of the ways Christians can understand our sexuality while remaining faithful.

In part two, I turn to the concept of vocation in more depth. What is vocation? How can you tell what yours is? And why does it matter? (This will also be where I explain why I'm not a nun, although I suspect I could rock a pantsuit.) I also discuss Christian community and its difficulties; devoted, sacrificial friendship as we see it in Christian history, theology, and contemporary practice; and why service to others is an area in which celibate gay people may have especial gifts to offer.

I also talk about common problems with faithful, chaste gay Catholic life. You wouldn't trust a marriage manual that was written as if nobody ever had to deal with fighting about money, childrearing, bad sex, or farting in bed. I want to be equally real about the challenges of celibate gay life, including loneliness, lack of accountability, and anger at the Church. I offer comfort and support, as well as describe ways in which I've sought to ease these struggles in my own life.

Finally, in the appendices, I give my take on the resources available to gay Christians today. I'll address the most common life-advice questions people bring to me when I do speaking engagements. And in appendix three, I offer suggestions for things you can do, no matter what your own orientation may be, to make the Church a more beautiful and welcoming home for gay or same-sex attracted Christians.

When we hear rhetoric of "healing" used about homosexuality in Christian contexts, I think we often assume that the speaker means that gay people should be healed *of their homosexuality*— turned straight. But my friend Ron Belgau noted that mature, spiritually fruitful celibacy requires its own forms of healing. We can think of *healing* as the process by which we are freed from self-obsession so that we can love others the way God is calling us to love.

Notes on Language

Throughout this book, I mostly use either *Christian* or *Catholic* when I mean "Christian who accepts that sex is only licit within heterosexual marriage." If I want to talk about Christians who reject what I suppose we must call the "traditional" teaching on human sexuality, I generally either name the denomination or use a long clunky phrase like the one I just wrote. I hope the concision I gain from using *Christian* or *Catholic* is not too off-putting to non-Catholic readers. I know many Protestants hold similar beliefs and face similar issues, and this is all the more true of Orthodox Christians, but since I am not steeped in those traditions myself, I thought it was better to speak from a Catholic perspective rather than trying to speak for everyone and accidentally misrepresent other churches. I also hope that Christians (including Catholics) who reject the "traditional" or Catholic view of human sexuality don't take offense at my word choice. I'm not questioning the depth of your faith, even though I disagree with the implications you draw from it in this area. I don't think people want to read a book that uses the phrase "accepts the belief that sexual activity is only licit within heterosexual marriage" on every single page.

I switch between the terms *gay, lesbian, queer,* and *same-sex attracted* more or less based on instinct. When I want to emphasize difference, alienation, or the radical vulnerability of the celibate, I probably say *queer;* when I want to talk about gay cultures or my own self-identification I mostly say *gay* or *lesbian;* when I want to speak specifically about eros directed at a member of one's own sex, without implying anything about involvement with or approval of contemporary gay culture, I'll try to remember to use *same-sex attracted.*

But please don't read too much into my choices here. The discussion of homosexuality within the Christian churches, at least in America, has become obsessed with finding the right identity label. An insouciance toward all of these labels—a certain lightness of touch, a willingness to accept all of them and reify none—would do us a lot of good. However, I've identified specific other people in the way they prefer. If somebody calls himself a man with same-sex attraction, it's not my place to say that he's "really" gay.

And now, come! We are ready for the floor show!

part one

Coming Out
Catholic

chapter one
A Charmed Life

I was born in Madison, Wisconsin, the younger daughter of two law professors. (My mother later became a prisoners' rights lawyer, first with the American Civil Liberties Union and then under her own shingle.)

When I was three, my family moved to Washington, DC. While our neighborhood was not exactly a Ray Bradbury small-town idyll (our house was broken into and our car stolen, both more than once), it was still the kind of place where packs of children roamed freely in and out of kitchens and backyards under the watchful eyes of the local grandmas. My childhood memories have a lot of lilacs in them, honeysuckle, hand-clap rhymes, double Dutch, poodle-shaped pink barrettes, watermelon on the Fourth of July, and pretending to be an Alaskan husky driver—or sometimes an Alaskan husky—when I had to walk to school in the snowy depths of February.

I was, and perhaps remain, a fairly stereotypical youngest child (of two), irresponsible, diva-esque, and often oblivious to others' needs. Nonetheless, my childhood was basically lovely. My parents had and still have a strong marriage. In elementary school, I usually had a gang of girls to play with. I was teased a bit for being a genuinely weird kid. (I explained that I would change my name to Zilla when I grew up, which got me the obvious Japanese monster-movie nickname, and said that I had a special destiny and could see visions of the future.) But I was never bullied and was generally even protected from the usual childhood fights. I think I was very self-centered, in the way that privileged children often are, because the adults in my life protected me from their troubles rather than forcing too much responsibility on me at a young age. I don't remember ever being punished by my parents, not once—not because I was spoiled, and definitely not because I always behaved, but because the mere expression of disapproval was usually enough to make me genuinely sorry. (For about an hour, at least. I was a pretty mercurial kid.)

I was born with life-threatening birth defects, which were detected when I was an infant. The main problem was that a blood vessel had gone rogue, wrapping itself around my trachea so I couldn't breathe. At the time, only two hospitals in the country would perform the necessary surgeries on a six-month-old, so my parents and I flew to Boston Children's, whose doctors saved my life. For a little more than half of the next year I breathed through a tube, which my parents had to clean and care for. Everyone in my family suffered through this period, not knowing whether I was going to make it.

Out of all of us, I suffered the least by far. I don't remember any of this. In later years I got bronchitis and pneumonia a lot— about once a year until I was in college—and while my fevers and deep coughing frightened my mother, I saw my illnesses as a week off of school in which I could reread Diana Wynne Jones and watch *The Mysterious Cities of Gold* on Nickelodeon. The stress my mom felt when I was sick was hard for me to understand because I had never experienced the fear that I wouldn't get better. I only learned about what my parents and sister had undergone on my behalf—the stress my birth defects had put on each of them individually, and on the family—gradually, and many years later.

I didn't think of myself as a "happy" or "unhappy" child. I don't think most children consider themselves in those terms. I knew I had a terrible temper, was pretty poorly behaved, and lied a lot. I also felt smart and was confident in my abilities in school and, for the most part, in my friendships.

It's easy to get defensive in describing one's childhood. At one point I asked an online forum to recommend memoirs concerning alcoholism or addiction in which the writer came from a basically loving, happy, and stable family, and the response I got was, "Have you tried looking under 'fiction'?" But this response is based on a misconception. Two misconceptions, really. First of all, if you'd like an answer to my question you can check out David Carr's terrific memoir, *The Night of the Gun: A Reporter Investigates the Darkest Story of His Life—His Own*. One reason I love this book is precisely that although addiction runs in Carr's family, and not in mine, his upbringing was basically loving and supportive. But the idea that no kids from "good homes" end up addicted is based on a much deeper misunderstanding. Good parenting can't in all cases prevent addiction. Parents can sometimes make the fall shorter and the landing softer, but they can't keep their kids from ever falling down.

In many respects my childhood was about as good as childhood gets. There was a rougher undercurrent of loneliness and a certain insecurity that caused me to seesaw between self-aggrandizing fantasy and intense self-blame. I'm not sure that I felt these things more deeply or frequently than other children (Harriet the Spy goes through some tough times), but it's interesting that most of my actual memories of childhood have some element of unhappiness or loneliness.

One moment, which was repeated many times throughout my childhood and which I came to consider central to my sense of self, captures my uncertainty about my place in the world. In this composite memory, it's a hot summer afternoon, with the air honeyed and humid. I'm in my bedroom playing with the toys I kept on top of my dresser drawer: a village of miniature unicorns, rag dolls, and china salt-and-pepper shakers shaped like cats. Some of these dolls and knickknacks had recurring characters (there was one teddy bear who was usually a lady pirate and a doll who was usually a sort of trickster), but the story lines varied wildly depending on what I'd been reading. Only one toy was fixed to a specific storyline—the exiled soldier.

The soldier was a tiny unpainted tabletop figure, which I think I found in someone's backyard. He was a waxy yellow, with blurry features and a yellow base to keep him upright. His story always began after its major precipitating event: He had committed some great crime, for which he was exiled from the tchotchke village. He had to stand at the edge of the dresser, facing away from the other knickknacks, guarding the village that had cast him out; he was not even allowed to look back at his home.

I can't remember what I thought he might have done. I think the crime itself shifted around at random, since it didn't seem to matter. It was a bad enough crime that he accepted exile as a fitting punishment, and although in some versions of the story he began by feeling great bitterness toward the villagers, over time his resentment softened, and he grew to love them and even find solace in his task of protecting them.

At last, one day, a threat came to the village. A giant polar bear! A purple dragon! A whole Lego army! Whatever it was, the plastic soldier set his face valiantly against the threat and defended the village with all his tiny might. Often, he died in the attempt. About half the time, whether he survived or not, I allowed him release from his punishment: The villagers recognized his penitence and valor, and either welcomed him back home or at least forgave him enough to bury him within the grounds of the village rather than on the cliff's side. The other half of the time I indulged my more depressive or cynical tendencies and made the villagers ungrateful and unable to recognize that the criminal had become a hero.

There are a lot of things I could say about this childhood story that so attracted me. For one thing, it's pretty obvious that I read Edward Everett Hale's *Man Without a Country* at an impressionable age. But I also felt a deep identification with this story of conflicted belonging and alienation, guilt and penitence, exile and longing for a home one can't even see and can barely remember. For me, this story of the exiled soldier—the underlying loneliness and alienation it expressed, which lay alongside my sociability and strong friendships—is a part of my coming-out story and, eventually, a part of my conversion story.

Because I did feel a lack in myself, I felt some difference from the other children around me. I felt very keenly that something had gone *wrong*, that I was not who I should be or where I should be, and that this wrongness was in some way my own responsibility; it belonged to me, rather than just being something that had been done to me with no participation of my own. I toyed with various possible explanations over the years. When I was little, I considered that I might possibly be a changeling or an amnesiac alien spy. (This is what happens when you give a child with a bad conscience a library card.)

For this reason, coming out as gay was a huge relief to me. I do know that's not how most people feel. But in middle school, I "borrowed" (stole) from my sister a book with a lesbian protagonist. I read the description of a long-legged blonde Southern girl putting her boots up on a table. And I realized that the narrator felt about this noir-esque blonde the same way I felt about the curly-haired girl in my English class, the one with the cupid's-bow lips and the New York fashion sense. I felt like a lock finally finding its key, turning and opening. At last, my sense

of difference or alienation was explained. I wasn't an alien or a
changeling or just, you know, an idiot. I was gay.

A quiet, persistent voice remained, warning me, *You haven't
explained everything*. But it seemed to me that I had explained
enough. I came out to myself when I was about thirteen and came
out to my parents shortly after that.

I had been apprehensive about telling them. My parents had
gay friends (in fact, one of my mother's colleagues went on to
head what was then called the National Gay and Lesbian Task
Force), but I did realize that it was different when it was your
own daughter. My mom did her best not to say that this was "just
a phase," even though, frankly, everything about my personality
up to that time showed that I went through personae and obses-
sions as if the whole world were my costume closet. She said,
sort of joking but not really, "Well, we still expect you to give
us grandchildren!" She was obviously worried that I would be
attacked or discriminated against. (I was already a *girl*, though,
so a life in which I wasn't a target wasn't an option.) This might
have been the first time since the crisis of my infancy when she
had to seriously reassess the hopes and dreams she'd had for my
future. Letting go of that hope-infused image of one's children is
one of the hardest things any parent goes through, and parents
whose children come out typically have to let go of some very
specific ideas about what their children's futures will look like.

It's a hard thing for parents to accept, and gay children need
to be flexible and forgiving—we sometimes need to give up our
own fantasies of perfect parents—but I don't think we need to
blame ourselves for "burdening" our parents with the knowledge
of our sexuality. Most gay people I know wrestled for a long time
about whether or not to tell their parents, guilty and afraid that
they would shatter their parents' hopeful image of their child. But
letting go of the image of their perfect future child is one of the

most important parts of parenting. That's true for *every* parent. There are only two classes of parents who are spared this pain: the ones who refuse to do it, preferring to hurt their children and themselves by retreating into the fantasy that they can control who their children become, and the ones whose children never grow up. Neither of these situations is enviable.

chapter two
The Botany Club

In general, I was raised in a gay-accepting culture, or subculture. On the one hand, I was teased a bit in middle school by a guy who thought it was hilarious to gabble, "Lesbosaywhat?" so that you'd say, ". . . What?" A girl at a summer program I attended refused to room with me because I was gay—although my new roommate became one of my closest friends, so I think I won that round. And on the other hand, I went to a Quaker summer camp where the counselors introduced us to the lesbian country music group Two Nice Girls.

I attended a progressive private high school that, in 1992, was just starting to grapple with newly public queer students. On certain unlucky days, the teacher would wheel out the TV set and the VCR on a cart, and we all had to watch various *ABC Afterschool Special*–type videos about guidance-counselor issues. There was one about a girl who had breasts of two different sizes, whose angst was relieved when a fitting-room attendant flung aside all the *other* ladies' fitting-room curtains to reveal that breasts come in many different shapes and sizes. Our heroine was reassured, but I suspect the other ladies were not. The boy version of this story included a zookeeper who opened his reassurance monologue with the lines, "I see a lot of penises in my line of work, son! *Animal* penises, that is." Again, the hero responds with vulnerable honesty rather than, for example, shrieking and running.

And then there was the gay video. I don't remember what the gay kid's name was, but let's call him Stan since I don't know anyone named Stan so I won't feel bad about it. The gay kid was a boy, obviously, because male homosexuality is the first and often only kind this culture thinks about, and he was white, obviously. He was quiet and shy, I think, and the plot of the movie was that he developed a crush on the captain of the football team and then maybe killed himself?

I suspect a lot of people who went to very different schools are scowling at my description here: *Your school actively tried to teach you that homophobia is bad, and you're complaining that they did it with clichés?* That's a totally fair point. The school was genuinely trying. But I think Stan's story may illustrate some of the dangers of trying to help the gay students without actually *asking* any of the people you're trying to help what they might want. We might very well disagree among ourselves, but that diversity of opinion would look very different from the monolithic pity narratives dreamt up by well-meaning heteros. The gay kid with a crush on Stereotypical Masculinity is a cliché—and a damaging one, since it can reinforce ideas that homosexuality is a form of projected longing for the masculinity one feels that one lacks. The gay teen suicide, while clearly a real and terrible phenomenon, can become a self-fulfilling prophecy of despair if that's the only story we ever tell. I don't think Stan's story was meant to make actual gay kids feel worthwhile or hopeful. I think it was meant to make straight kids feel bad for teasing us.

Contrast this with a story created by actual gay people. Around the same time our school had us watch the tale of Stan, my best friend, Jason, and I saw a movie called *The Disco Years* at a local gay film festival. The hero of this movie was also a white guy. He may have even had a crush on a popular and stereotypically masculine kid, but I can't remember. What I do remember is that he was a fully imagined character with an inner life, who existed for his own purposes and not to inspire important emotions in straight kids. He was bitchy (when a girl teased him he snapped, "At least I don't look like a Valley Girl who dresses in the dark!"), he wasn't a role model, and he felt real. I doubt even the hippest guidance counselor could have gotten away with showing this movie in the classroom. But the places where we heard gay stories told *in gay voices* were so much more raw—and so much more hopeful—than a soothing Hallmark card about tolerance.

I tell this story for two reasons. One, to give some context for the liberal subculture in which I was raised. And two, in high school my friends and I used the slogan "Don't cover my face with your heart." In other words, don't trade the difficult work of listening to and engaging with actual queer people for the easy work of pitying us. Straight people on both sides of the "Does the Christian faith bar gay sex?" question often tell themselves self-comforting fables in which the allegorical figure of the homosexual replaces actual gay people. On one side, the allegorical homosexual experiences his sexuality purely as a wound, dealt to him by those childhood nightmares, which a queer Christian friend of mine sardonically named "Farther" and "Smother." On the other side, allegorical homosexuals are all united in their belief that gay marriage and bourgeois normalcy are the only alternatives to suicide. This gives straight people an easy way to do good: By standing up for an "inclusive" Gospel, they can polish their own righteousness without facing uncomfortable challenges to their own beliefs about marriage, sexual fidelity, gender, celibacy, or whether mere normalcy should ever be a Christian norm. The fables make it impossible for the well-meaning straight people to *see* the objects of their gentle emotions.

The encounters of these pious fables with real gay people are often tense. Perhaps this is part of why even our progressive, Stan-supporting high school didn't agree to the one request their actual gay students were in fact making, which was permission to form a gay-straight alliance.

One of the seniors had tried to start a gay-straight alliance the year before Jason and I were freshmen but had been rebuffed by the administration. The administration argued, first, that students shouldn't be "forced" to think about questions of sexual orientation or pick an identity (which was a bit tough to hear if you felt that you'd been forced to think about it all on your own) and, second, that the school was already a safe and welcoming space for gay students.

This was truer than it would have been in most places. One of the reasons I don't accept the claim that bullying is just an inevitable part of childhood—"kids will be kids" and all that—is that *none* of the schools I've attended had bullying problems. And in almost every story I've heard from people who were severely bullied as children, a recurring theme is the indifference of adults in authority, generally either teachers, parents, or both. These adults *knew* and did nothing or even blamed the child for attracting cruelty. They abandoned the bullied kids. This abandonment not only allows bullying to continue but also deepens the child's feeling of worthlessness. In the schools I attended, the teachers seemed to care if we respected one another. They didn't interfere in minor schoolyard teasing, but I never got the impression that any kind of physical or sustained emotional targeting would be acceptable. This was true of my public elementary school, my private middle school, and the progressive private high school, which prided itself on its ability to support its gay students without acknowledging our existence. In my years at that high school, I only heard of two incidents I would consider attempts at bullying by attack or intimidation.

The thing is—the reason the administration's position seemed naïve to us at best and callous at worst—those two exceptions both happened to openly gay students because they were gay. One was a little gang of mini-thugs who tried to attack a gay kid with hockey sticks while shouting slurs, if I recall correctly. In the other case, a senior-class lesbian went to a party where she was cornered by a group of boys from our school who promised that they were going to teach her a lesson. Both kids escaped unharmed, but even so, it was clear that homosexuality was the one thing for which you could and would be taunted, threatened, and attacked, even at the safest school.

So we didn't take no for an answer, and we built a sort of underground network of gay students. We joked that we would call ourselves the Botany Club: Our first order of business would be the study of pansies. Our school couldn't actually control whether or not it had a gay students' group. It could only choose whether the group was public or whether it was an underground, private clique, which considered itself inherently antagonistic to the school administration.

I found my first girlfriend through that network. She was a senior and I was a freshman, and I *acted* like a freshman too. I was trying to be queer in the right way, to like the right bands and the right books. Fortunately, my friends were able to quash this conformist nonconformity. When I said something like, "How can you not like k.d. lang? What kind of a bisexual *are* you?" they looked at me until I felt very gauche, although I defensively replied, "What? I was just joking!"

I tried to have a girlfriend the right way too. The first time we kissed, I said "I love you" afterward because I thought that was what you were supposed to do when you kissed someone. She laughed a little, a husky fluttering laugh like a bird bathing in dust, paused, and said, "Yeah . . ."

But does it matter how much of what I felt was "authentic," if I felt it so deeply that it shook me? We'd go up to my room and play her cassette tapes and make out, and afterward I'd watch as she drove away, and I would shiver. The first time, I had to kneel when she was gone, too overwhelmed to stand. All of that was real.

She was very patient with me. She was beautiful and shy, and I was awkward and loud, and it shouldn't have been too surprising that she broke up with me because, she said, she didn't want to be as far out of the closet as I was.

* * * *

She graduated. Eventually we got permission to form an aboveground gay-straight alliance, which we gave the depressingly perky name "The Rainbow Coalition." Jason and I continued to be self-indulgent radicals who were very into being "queer." Although in his defense, I was tackier about it than he was. We put up posters no one understood and alienated the gay and lesbian teachers who would have been our natural allies. He was definitely my closest friend, but throughout high school, I had a big, shifting group of friends, most of whom were punks. On the way to school, I'd transform myself: hike up my skirt, spike my hair with a hotel bottle of shampoo, apply black lipstick without a mirror, and slip on fingerless gloves and a spiked dog collar. These were fashion fast-forward touches my mother had nixed, like the tutu ("I'm just worried that people will think you're mentally ill") and the jeans I spent an hour modifying so that they were a cyberpunk wonderland of wires and duct-tape patches. Jason sometimes wore fangs. We read magazines with pictures of glossy vampires wilting against cemetery crosses, lots of pin-ups of St. Sebastian (this is old-school!), and of course dyed black Shetland-pony hair.

There were a couple guys besides Jason, but most of us were girls. The idea that gay people lack a proper understanding of same-sex friendship has always struck me as implausible because I've always had a lot of female friends. I thought most of my friends were attractive but didn't actually fall for them, although I admit that I spent very little time drawing a line between eros and friendship. I mostly wanted to scatter glitter over that line. In high school I had another much more serious relationship with a girl, and one dumb-fun hookup session, which involved body painting and plastic goblets of wine.

I went to meetings of the Sexual Minority Youth Assistance League (SMYAL), where I was reminded that most queer teenagers were not primarily worried about what color their fishnets should be. I met a teen butch-femme couple, kids trying to stay on the high side of homelessness, and an ex-military guy, who was maybe six years older than me and who talked about nursing his boyfriend through the last stages of AIDS. Later I started going to Riot Grrrl meetings out in Arlington, Virginia. Riot Grrrl was, by that time, much more heavily middle- and upper-class than SMYAL and *much* more white. It was also the first place I ever heard girls talk openly about being sexually abused, about overcoming or struggling with eating disorders, and about hating themselves as well as other girls and trying to transform that hatred into love and courage.

This is my last note for a while on how terrific my parents are, but I will say that because I never learned to drive, my father drove me to SMYAL, to Riot Grrrl, and to church. This was pretty intensely above and beyond.

One reason I continue to "identify as" gay is that gay communities were places where I learned to be less self-centered. They were places where I encountered beauty and learned solidarity and humility.

They were also places where I found a sense of belonging. One reason I fell in love with the band the Smiths after my first girlfriend gave me a dubbed cassette tape of their first album is that front man Morrissey is great at ferreting out, honoring, and identifying himself with queer Catholic predecessors: Wilde, Pasolini, and Visconti. This was an impulse I had very deeply. I spent hours rewinding and replaying cassette tapes, trying to glimpse through the lyrics someone who felt the way I did— someone who loved in the unusual, coded, flamboyant-then-hidden, *queer* way I did. For the girl without a country, discovering the Smiths and Jean Genet and Derek Jarman felt like coming home.

The hungry search for queer stories expanded my worldview. I read Dorothy Allison and discovered a picture of a childhood that was in some ways painfully different from mine—a childhood of poverty and abuse—but in other ways startlingly recognizable. She wrote about the shattering emotional rush of finding one's life reflected in literature, finally being able to live in the world "not as a stranger."[1] She gave that hope to me.

Many theories of homosexuality posit a certain narcissism at its heart. If *la difference*, sexual difference, is the greatest and most meaningful difference within human nature, then seeking sexual union with someone on "your side" of that dividing line seems like a rejection of solidarity. It seems like a rejection of difference and a clinging to one's own kind. Every heterosexual union is xenophiliac: a fraught concord of sexual strangers, a meeting with the Other. This is one reason heterosexual union is so often used to symbolize the human encounter with God; God is the ultimate Other, whom we must love as deeply and incarnationally as a man should love his wife.

I accept several of the premises of this claim. I agree that *la difference* is not like other differences; it is deeper and more sublime. I agree that heterosexual union is unique because, as Maggie Gallagher has often said, it "brings together the two

halves of humanity"—and it does this even when the union is
childless. The union of man and woman is marked as unique in
the Bible even before humans begin to procreate. Adam and Eve
had no children until they left Eden, and yet when Pope John
Paul II looked for a biblical model of human sexuality, he found
none better than this childless couple's marital paradise. It is
the union of man and woman, not solely procreation, that the
Catholic Church's vision of sexuality exalts. Without resorting to
explicitly Christian language, we can say that *eros* may be most
interestingly defined as the ardent desire for union with one who
is—and remains—deeply different from oneself. In this more
classical understanding, too, homosexuality appears *less* erotic
and more inward-looking than heterosexuality.

And yet my actual experience of lesbian love suggests that
something is missing from these theories. I *did* feel that the
women I loved were the Other. They felt like *woman*, for whom I
yearned, and yet I did not experience the uncertainty or discom-
fort in my own gender, which ex-gay theories suggest I should
have felt. It seemed easy for me to simultaneously understand
myself as a woman and be erotically drawn to women as the
Other. They seemed strange and excitingly unpredictable, about
as far from mirror images as one could get.

I think it would take a great deal of sensitivity—probably
more than I possess—to tease out possible theoretical understandings that would reconcile my emotions and experiences
with my deep (and pre-conversion) belief in the unique importance and sublimity of sexual difference. I think it's possible that
when I loved women I did dis-gender myself to a certain extent,
thinking of myself more as an ardent or abject suitor, using primarily masculine role models.[2] It could be argued that while my
gender identity was firm enough to persist even in lesbian eros,
I ended up engaging in a kind of doublethink, in which woman

was Self until I needed her to be Other for erotic purposes. Or it could simply be said that no theory will ever fully capture everyone's experiences, and our loves will always unwind in complex tangles that not even poetry—let alone philosophy—can trace from end to end. There are many kinds of homosexuality, many styles, and mine may be one of the weirder ones. I don't want to offer a Grand Unified Theory of Lesbianism, or even of my own lesbianism; I want to give you some sense of what my experience feels like, and you can do with that information what you will.

But I do want to emphasize that narcissism, especially in the sense of selfishness and self-centeredness, was more or less the opposite of what I experienced in lesbian relationships. I could be a total drama queen, and as a result, the dissolution of my relationships was my fault most of the time, but I also genuinely liked to please and take care of the women I loved. I attended sickbeds and I cooked meals. (This sometimes led to major drama, as on the Night of the Screaming Sweet Potatoes: I *really* wanted to impress my girlfriend with my delicious vegetarian cooking—yes, I was a vegetarian lesbian; I also love cats—but my sweet potatoes wouldn't bake, and literally began to emit a high-pitched shriek as air escaped their rock-hard skins. The whole thing ended in tears.) Relationships, and even fleeting crushes, gave me much-needed practice in listening, trying to understand someone with a very different worldview, forgiving, and asking for forgiveness. I've gone on to use these skills in my friendships, but lesbianism is part of the arena in which I learned them. This is another reason I continue to call myself gay: being in love with women has usually made me a better person.

And finally, being clear about the beauty and guidance I found in gay communities may make it obvious that what I found in the Church was even greater. Many people come to Christ in some degree of desperation, fleeing a way of life that feels like a trap. Their gratitude is often humbling and inspiring. But it's an equally, if differently, powerful case for Christ to say that his beauty and truth are overwhelming even for someone who has already found a good-enough, livable place in the world.

* * * *

In high school I had my introduction to Catholicism—sort of. Jason was raised Catholic but didn't practice; I regarded the Church as a weird mix of oppressive and exotic. I got to tag along when the Latin classes in our school went to Italy over spring break. I remember being enthralled by the reliquaries—I loved the Gothic sensuality that led people to honor and adorn the bones of the beloved dead—and disgusted by a huge, gory statue of St. Sebastian, which stretched over our heads in one church like a sky made of corpse. I thought of Catholicism as vivid and visceral but also sex hating, body hating, and life hating. When our tour guide described St. Peter turning back to go to Rome even though he knew he would be martyred there, I hissed to Jason, *"That's* pretty Catholic!" Knowing that I meant it as an insult (Catholics are stupid and prefer death to life), he stuck his tongue out at me; and yet I'm pretty sure I was the childish one in that conversation.

Catholicism was mostly queer to me: Jarman's *Caravaggio,* Wilde's *Salome.* It was attractive in a glamour-of-evil kind of way. It was thrilling in a way that the local Baptists weren't—but it was also more threatening than them, more dedicated, as I saw it, to crushing gay liberation and women's rights, not just in the United States but worldwide. I wrote a short story called "The Church Is the Body" in which—not knowing the extent to which I was echoing Catholic language and even, in a distorted way, Catholic theology—I exalted the sick and weakened body of a woman cast out by her local, disgustingly healthy, low-church

Protestant congregation. Actually believing and practicing a religion, however, was totally alien to me and not even a real enough
option to be frightening.

* * * *

The final introduction I received in high school was to alcohol. I'd had champagne at weddings and the occasional wine
or beer with friends, but the first time I ever got drunk was at
a cast party for one of the school plays. It should have been an
amazingly embarrassing experience: I was *that* girl, the one who
finished the dregs of other people's beers and sloppily made out
with quasi-bisexual guys she didn't even like. And yet on the
Metro going home the next morning, curving high up against the
low-slung District skyline, I felt exhilarated. I felt scoured and
somehow new. I felt proud of myself for not being ashamed. (This
is what you get when you take Sir John Falstaff as a role model!)
Getting drunk and acting stupid made me feel young, alive, and
weirdly self-accepting. I felt deliciously, deliriously impure and
ready for more.

The guy I'd "kissed" (licked) was too embarrassed to even
look at me at school on Monday. I grinned at him and sailed on
blithely. The moment at which these things go from "crazy night"
to "public humiliation" is the moment when most people stop
drinking so much.

I didn't actually drink too frequently back then. I'm not sure I
drank more than a few times before college, although each time,
I drank to get drunk. When I drank I felt sparklier and smarter.
There's a moment in *Alice in Wonderland* in which Alice can't
remember a simple childhood rhyme, and she begins to fear that
she isn't Alice at all but rather Mabel, the slowest child in her
class. When I was drinking, I never worried that I was Mabel.
I didn't like the taste—I was drinking forties of Olde English

malt liquor here, representing my derelict hometown as best I could—but I loved the effects.

And there was a romance about alcohol, about the ecstasy it provoked. It could take you outside the confines of your ordinary experience and your too-familiar self. Caroline Knapp titled her alcoholism memoir *Drinking: A Love Story,* and one lesson I took away from her book is that if you have a *relationship* with alcohol, you might have a problem with alcohol. I had a major, starry-eyed crush.

* * * *

Right before I started college, I was drifting. I'm very easily dissatisfied, and although I had found a good place to be, I still felt something was lacking. Senior year of high school had been kind of a train wreck. I broke up with my girlfriend for reasons that were ninety percent my own self-righteousness. My larger friendship group splintered. I spent the summer reading Shakespeare, listening to hip-hop on the radio late at night, and wondering who I would be a year later.

"Almost Catholic" was not one of the many possible answers I entertained.

chapter three

Evidence for the Prosecution

In the first week of freshman year, a friend of mine said he and his roommate were going to check out some kind of right-wing debate society and noted, "They have free mixed drinks!" I figured that was enough to justify a couple hours gawking at zoo animals. (Actually, I probably respected zoo animals more than I respected conservatives. I doubt that I believed zoo animals should be locked up.) I headed into this debate in hot pink fishnets, a tiger-print skirt held together with safety pins and lies, and a Boy Scout T-shirt, clutching a book by Sister Souljah. A bemused, shambolic junior with a Viking beard mixed me a vodka and Coke. It tasted a little bit like ground glass, but then, Olde English tastes a little bit like a garbage man's strike, so we've established that I wasn't choosy.

I ended up in a long argument with one of the zoo animals, a Catholic divinity school student. I was arguing that literature was better than philosophy because of relativism. He mounted a strong defense of objective truth and philosophy as a form of love, an eros for truth. I would tell you more about it but my memory is a bit slushy. Whatever he said intrigued me enough that I made sure to tell one of the group's officers, "This is *definitely* an organization I want to join!"

This did not appear to thrill them. But the more I got to know them, the more they broke my stereotypes of callous, dumb right-wingers. They told me about their own seeking, their own

conversions (both to and from various religions), and the difficulties those changes in belief had caused in their lives.

Here I met the first Catholics who actually evangelized me.
They disabused me of some of my many misconceptions about
the Church. For example, I had thought of *sin* as a synonym for
shame. I thought anyone who talked about sin was using the term
to draw a line between the good people and the bad ones, the
sheep and the goats. I was pretty sure I was a goat, and I was glad
of it. I had no desire to join the sheep clique. But the Catholics I
met suggested that I already knew what sin felt like—even what
original sin felt like.

Original sin, they said, was that conflict in the self, that self-di-
vision in which we're alienated from our best impulses. It's the
name we give our reverse heliotropism, the longing to do wrong
and the glee or relief we sometimes feel when we go against our
own consciences. It's the imp of the perverse, as Edgar Allan
Poe would say, or the inner voice of hatred and rejection rather
than love.

As for sin itself, I could begin by thinking of it as wrongdoing—gossip, cruelty, obliviousness to others' suffering. All of
these were wrong and I'd done all of them, so I already knew
what sin was. But they pointed out that *sin* was actually a much
more hopeful concept than simple wrongdoing. *Wrongdoing*
implies no particular narrative, whereas *sin* comes from a religious tradition that insists on the possibility of redemption. Far
from implying an indelible stain, sin implies the possibility of
salvation.

This understanding of sin is only one angle from which my
friends presented the Church to me. There were other questions,
such as where poetic meaning comes from. When you read the
work of an author who has found the exact image for what she
wants to convey, is that sense of *rightness* and harmony between

image and meaning imposed on objects in the world by the human creator? Does the poet draw from a symbolic alphabet created and limited by his or her culture? Or does the poet simply recognize a meaning inherent in the objects themselves?

I had casually believed, as a default position, that objects in the world each had an inherent meaning. When I was writing and I hit upon the right image, I didn't think that I was simply imposing my own personal awesomeness on the world, molding it like Play-Doh until it took on the shapes I needed to convey my meaning. I was closer to believing that meaning is culturally relative, that the difference between a sparrow and a vulture is imposed by human culture and *that's* why Shakespeare didn't write, "There is a special providence in the fall of a vulture."[1] (Although wouldn't it have been fierce if he had?)

Both of these explanations for the poetic meaning of images are partly true. It's true that artists contribute to our sense of what images, objects, animals *mean* and what they can do in future artworks. It's also true that culture shapes our sense of what is the appropriate or poetically perfect image. But there seemed to me to be something beyond both of these sources of meaning. After all, if I am the one imposing meaning on a sparrow, it can never mean anything greater than what I can imagine or allow it to mean. If my culture imposes meaning on it, it can never be greater than what my culture can imagine. We end up confined in our own skins or, at best, our own time and place, never actually touching the vivid outside reality of the object or image itself.

Moreover, I was not convinced that poetic meaning was simply created rather than recognized. It *felt* like recognition. When I nodded at Shakespeare's line about the sparrow, it felt like I was responding to a fact about sparrows, not just to facts about Shakespeare and Elizabethan culture and the influence of the Bible. I believed that you could let a sparrow be a sparrow, not just a

collage of pasted-together scraps of culture and allusion, and
still believe it was the only right image for your play or poem.

When I tried to figure out where this inherent meaning might
come from, it was hard to guess. There seemed to be no mean-
ing-infusing entity available *other* than individual humans and
human cultures. G. K. Chesterton's *The Dumb Ox: St. Thomas
Aquinas* suggested the possibility that what I was noticing was
the fingerprint of the Creator God:

> That strangeness of things, which is the light in all poetry, and
> indeed in all art, is really connected with their otherness; or
> what is called their objectivity. . . . According to Aquinas, the
> object becomes a part of the mind; nay, according to Aquinas,
> the mind actually becomes the object. But, as one commentator
> acutely puts it, it only becomes the object and does not create
> the object. In other words, the object is an object; it can and
> does exist outside the mind, or in the absence of the mind.
> And therefore it enlarges the mind of which it becomes a part.
> The mind conquers a new province like an emperor; but only
> because the mind has answered the bell like a servant. . . . For
> this feeding upon fact is itself; as an organ it has an object which
> is objective; this eating of the strange strong meat of reality.[2]

I'm not sure a conversion can be parsed or fully explained
any more than a love affair can. I can list influences—St. Anselm's
treatise on the Incarnation, *Cur Deus Homo*; that Aquinas biography by Chesterton (and his even better biography of St. Francis); the anthology of postmodern essays *Christianity in Jewish
Terms*, which helped me realize that the concepts of incarnation
and redemption were intensely important to me. I could tell you
about the conversations I had, but reading about conversations is
nothing like being a part of them. What I can tell you is that the
experience of becoming Catholic, recognizing the fingerprints of
the Catholic God on the world around me, felt very much like

the experience of coming out to myself. There were elements of falling in love—I found the Church alluring as well as confusing and threatening. There were also elements of recognizing truth. There was, above all, a sense that many of my longings and beliefs were converging on a single object.

That object was distinctly the Catholic God and not the Jewish one. I had received a smattering of Jewish religious education. I went to a Jewish summer day camp where we learned prayers, ate challah and drank grape juice on Shabbat, and played the game Pin the Beard on Mordecai. I had been to a handful of Jewish religious services, but my actual conversion experience was rooted in distinctively Christian concepts such as the Eucharist and the Crucifixion.

I remember one dinner-table debate between a Catholic junior, who eventually became my godfather, and a Jewish senior, who was at the start of a long process of transitioning from Jew-fro'd, pot-smoking libertarian to sukkah-dwelling, davening Hasid. This Jew is one of the smartest people I've ever met. When people questioned him he'd lower his head, nod and listen closely, humbly, sometimes grinning and shaking his head slowly like a puzzled bear as he tried to understand the objection. One of our friends described a debate with him this way: "We asked him, 'How can we find the source of ethics?' And he said, 'Consult the wise.' So we asked him, 'How can we find the source of ethics?' And he said, 'Consult the wise.' So we asked *him* . . . !" That's the esteem in which we held him, and for good reason.

But he lost this argument, one of maybe two I ever saw him lose. He was arguing against what I later learned was St. Anselm's account of the Incarnation. The short version is that humans, having separated ourselves from God through sin, can't by our own power restore ourselves to a condition of perfect spiritual health. (Try it, you'll see.) And yet we have a responsibility to do so. We need justice, maybe even long for it in the way that children sometimes feel that they need some kind of punishment when they've done wrong, or else they feel bereft and anchorless. We need justice, and yet we can't bear it.

The Incarnation cuts through this Gordian knot. Jesus is one of us, not merely man but almost a Platonic form of Man. And yet because he is also God, his sacrifice can be infinite and free in a way ours cannot be. With the Incarnation and then the Crucifixion, the words of the psalm are fulfilled: "Righteousness and peace have kissed each other" (Ps 85:10).

There are some big gaps in the argument as presented here. I encourage you to seek out St. Anselm's treatise if it interests you (and if you have a taste for Christian neo-Platonism, since you need a good stomach for that if you want to read St. Anselm at all). Some of these gaps are easy to fill in once you understand more about Christian practice. For example, you may ask: Even if Jesus is sort of Ultimate Man, what does that have to do with *me?* How can his sacrifice be applied to me as if I did it myself?

As I understand it, we enter into Christ's sacrifice when we accept God's will for us and take up our own crosses, whatever they may be. We unite our own sufferings to Christ. We share in his cross and, by doing so, prepare ourselves to share in his heaven. So Jesus does not pay our debts without our consent; we must act on our side by accepting God's love and surrendering to it, whatever it may demand of us. St. Paul said in Colossians that believers "fill up . . . what is lacking in the afflictions of Christ" (Col 1:24). Fr. Thomas Hopko makes the point in his *Christian Faith and Same-Sex Attraction*: "I once asked my professor of theology, Serge S. Verkhovskoy, what could possibly be lacking in Christ's sufferings and afflictions for the sake of our salvation. His answer was, 'Our personal participation in them.'"[3]

What appealed to me most about St. Anselm's argument as presented by my godfather-to-be was that it didn't shy away from the need for justice but also acknowledged that justice was totally unsustainable for mere humans. I already believed that, and it was the source of a lot of my guilt and anxiety. I already believed that *justice* meant getting what you deserved. That could play out in "social justice" terms, where justice would mean that poor or oppressed people got a much better deal than their present conditions. But justice also entailed the punishment of wrongdoers, and I was pretty sure that I was mostly not oppressed but mostly a wrongdoer. I knew the world needed justice and that I needed it in my own life, but I didn't think I could bear it.

I mistrusted mercy because it seemed like an excuse, "forgive and forget," let's pretend this never happened. It seemed like taking an eraser to one's life, which not only made my actions meaningless but also meant that reconciliation could only be achieved on the basis of falsehood. Seeing that justice and mercy could be united, rather than mercy simply overruling justice as if justice didn't matter, helped me to begin to long for mercy as I longed for justice. It wasn't so much that the "mathematics" of St. Anselm's syllogisms went through. It was more that he gave me permission to yearn for mercy.

Through all these arguments and spiritual shifts, I had reached the point where I believed that if there were a god, it was probably the Catholic one. I darkly suspected that the world might be the work of that bloody-minded God. I began to pray, kneeling beside my dorm-room bed, feeling like an idiot. It is instructively humiliating to pray, and for that reason, I think praying on one's knees or in some other posture of submission is almost always preferable. I continued to struggle with the arguments during the daytime, and then at night I would pray.

And nothing happened.

My father tells this terrific joke about an old Jewish man who prays every day by the Wailing Wall in Jerusalem. In good times and in bad, even as the fighter jets roared over his head, this old man would go and pray, touching the sacred wall. A younger man who watched him admired his faith. One day this young man asked him, "What does it feel like to have such deep devotion that you can pray even in these difficult times?"

The old man answered, "It feels like I'm talking to a freaking wall!"

I shouldn't whine or compare my situation to this old man. I prayed for about two weeks in a kind of hideously embarrassed frigidity. That isn't actually a long time. I know many people who have pursued God with greater sincerity for much longer and have not received an answer they could perceive.

But I will say that the Jewish joke is comforting to me. I think many people reach a point at which their fundamental beliefs *imply* God but nonetheless resist the surrender of faith, thinking of themselves as agnostics because they haven't had a specific kind of emotional experience of God or encounter with God. They haven't had what in Catholic jargon would be called *consolations*—feelings of God's nearness or tenderness. And yet I think that they have had experiences of God, just not particularly warm ones. Your thoughts, questions, and beliefs are things you experience. God sometimes adorns our faith with consolations, and sometimes he removes those consolations, but the consolations themselves are not the substance of faith and should not be confused with faith. Don't wait for the God-lightning to strike you before you accept that you're a believer.

Now and then I do have a deep sense of God as Creator. I will be caught suddenly in a suspended moment, and it's as if I am cupped in his hands. Or it will seem that I see through the world as it appears, to the pulsing veins of blood and sinew: I see the

Crucifixion shining through the apparent world, always present. This focus on the Crucifixion has been a pretty constant feature of my own spirituality. It doesn't need to be central to yours in the same way. I find that the Crucifixion makes the Christian story believable, makes it match the world I see outside my window. The Crucifixion is violent and lurid; it's agonizing in the way the world is agonizing. A gentler, less tabloid-headline story would seem out of place in a violent world. But I have many friends who feel closer to the resurrected Christ and, as I've said, I also feel a pretty strong sense of God as Creator. Regardless of which moment in the life of Christ I perceive a special connection to, these sensations or emotions are not faith. They might be moments of special insight or moments of a specific kind of grace, but faith is a more persevering thing.

Nonetheless, I may have needed a moment of this kind of consolation in order to admit that I believed. For whatever reason, God chose to give me a powerful and unexpected feeling of his creating and sustaining presence. (Oddly enough it was just presence, not love—I don't think those two terms are truly separate in God, but since the aspect of love wasn't particularly relevant to me at that moment, it felt more like simple presence.) He chose to do this in the most bottom-shelf way possible. I was tipsy in a Yale bathroom, when I noticed a stain on the tiled wall. As I looked at it, it began to seem like a stain in a poem, probably a poem by T. S. Eliot since he was always good at making broken things significant. The stain had its own beauty, its own deep meaning. I felt that *click-click-click* of the tumblers turning and my heart unlocking.

I mean, feel free to laugh! This is one of those moments that work in individual lives, and possibly in fiction, but which I don't think come across in a mere memoir. But even in the sober light of day, I couldn't argue away the impression I'd received. I had found the Creator for whom I had, only recently, been looking. I actually like that God chose to reveal himself to me in this way. Mother Theresa said, "There is no humility without humiliation," and the truly humble circumstances of my conversion have a stupidity I find charming and clarifying. I also like that God used my weakness for alcohol to bring me to him. God uses whatever we give him.

My conversion wasn't linear. It felt more like making progress in your emotional life: constant backsliding, self-doubt, renewal of hope, realization that you're haring down the wrong path, trying again a different way—a long series of increasingly insistent surrenders. The bathroom thing happened in late spring of my freshman year, I think, but after a summer of scaring my parents by reading Chesterton in public, I wasn't sure what I believed. I started Rite of Christian Initiation of Adults (RCIA), aka catechism class, in the fall of my sophomore year. On the first day, the priest said matter-of-factly, "So, everyone here is going to be confirmed at Easter, right?" And although I had intended to keep my options open, I felt as though I had accepted conversion behind my own back—I was ready to say yes. That's how it looks in retrospect, of course. I do remember thinking at the time, *Yes!*, and being surprised by myself. But of course there's no way of knowing how I would tell this story if I'd changed my mind.

That year I also dated a guy, an atheist. It was weird (kissing a man was very strange although exciting in its own way, and the rules seemed to be different), and I behaved badly. I was clingy and self-centered. Every time I've thought I was interested in or in love with a man, I've fallen into self-dramatization and unrealistic fantasy, whereas with women I think I'm much more realistic and genuinely loving.

I was still very serious about identifying as queer. I tried to get my friends to explain the Church's teaching on homosexuality.

They had never raised the issue with me before, which showed great intuitive insight on their part. They answered the questions I was already asking, about larger concepts, such as guilt, forgiveness, art, and creation, rather than the questions the surrounding culture might have assumed I was interested in. They waited for me to raise the Gay Question.

This approach turned out to make me much more ready to hear what they had to say. I think if they'd assumed that they were "supposed to" witness to me by talking about God's plan for my sex life, I would have been put off by the arrogance of their assumptions: assumptions that they knew better than me which questions were important to my spiritual life and assumptions that they as well-meaning straight people understood homosexuality better than I did. When I did ask, I found their answers unsatisfactory; but then, they'd had the humility to do their best with a question *I* had pushed on *them*. I could respect that.

The guy who eventually became my godfather said that sex was like the Communion chalice. It wasn't just an ordinary cup and should only be used for the Blood of Christ; you shouldn't mix a giant mimosa in the thing. Communion with God, here, was analogous to the communion of man and woman in marriage. I thought that was a lovely analogy that did great honor to the body—and that also didn't actually answer the question. First of all, *why* was sex like the Communion chalice? There are other abilities that we can use both for the most sacred and the most secular purposes: We can use language to pray, for example, or to tell jokes, and both are fine by the Catholic Church. And second, why couldn't two women give themselves to each other in full communion? They could unite their bodies and their futures.

So I asked the priest who led our RCIA class. This guy is a patient, funny, hardworking Dominican; I think he's great. But his explanation was even less satisfying than my friend's. He tried to tell me that I already knew that lesbian sex was unnatural and wrong, because the parts don't fit. "It's like trying to open a door when the doorknob is wrapped in barbed wire," he said.

And, I mean, how did he *know*?

But beyond that question, obviously, I couldn't think of a worse analogy for lesbian sex. I'm not all "love between women is kittens and flowers," but barbed wire is a bit too kinky for me. And the notion of parts being designed for some uses and not others, in the absence of other moral constraints, didn't make a lot of sense to me. Our feet weren't "made" for figure skating. Our hands weren't "made" to talk with, and yet sign language exists. Even an activity like biting one's nails, while unwise and kind of gross, isn't immoral. So the idea that we could only use our reproductive organs for reproductive purposes struck me as weirdly mechanistic, treating the human body as a tool for self-replication: "factories that make factories," as the poet said.

I was faced with a choice. I didn't understand the Church's teaching on this issue, didn't like it, and suspected it might well be very relevant to my later life, especially if I broke up with the guy I was seeing (which in fact happened shortly after my Baptism). But I knew that even Thomas Aquinas couldn't understand everything about *God*. I couldn't demand perfect intellectual understanding from myself, even on issues close to my heart. Part of the reason we have a Church in the first place (only a part, but an important part) is so that we're not left to make up our own minds on every single issue. We're not left in the state an evangelical Protestant friend of mine self-deprecatingly described as, "So there we were, just me and Jesus . . ." with only the liturgy we like and only the morality we understand. The Church exists because even the saints need guidance and, often, correction.

So instead of asking myself whether I understood the reasoning behind the Church's teaching—the reasoning of God—I asked myself whether I was *more sure* that gay sex was morally neutral or more sure that the Catholic Church had the authority to teach sexual morality. And much to my surprise and dismay, I found that I was more sure of the second. I found that I was willing to accept the Church's teaching even when I didn't understand it. I began to prepare for Baptism.

The end of Lent in 1998 was tough. I knew that my parents and almost all of my friends were baffled and disappointed by my decision to become Catholic. Although I guess it's easy to caricature my life at that time as an extended exercise in teenage rebellion, in fact I valued my parents' good opinion highly and was not at all pleased to be going against what I had been taught. Even my closest friends found my decision completely opaque and tried to avoid the subject, which left me feeling very alone. I felt like an idiot every time I tried to explain myself. One of my relatives asked me how I could become Catholic given what the Church said about homosexuality. Instead of explaining my actual thinking, as I described it above, I stupidly tried to come up with some explanation and rambled something about procreation. "What about infertile couples?" she asked. Well, I said that in the Bible God had given some of those couples the blessing of a child, so he could presumably do that for infertile couples today. She replied, "So why can't he give a child to a gay couple?" I didn't have an answer. So that didn't exactly help my family understand where I was coming from.

During the Triduum (the three days preceding Easter Sunday: Holy Thursday, Good Friday, and Holy Saturday) my church held a series of talks on St. Edith Stein followed by eucharistic adoration. You'd think I would have been fascinated by St. Edith, the Jewish philosopher who became a Discalced Carmelite nun and was murdered in Auschwitz. But I remember absolutely nothing from the talks. I was too stressed out to focus.

I don't think I really understood why I was so stressed out; in fact, I doubt I understand it now. I'm generally a homebody who prefers old friends and old haunts, and Catholicism would make me alien to my family and most of my friends. I didn't think I'd be very good at being Catholic (I was right about that!), and I don't like being bad at things. But these psychological explanations are, I think, inadequate half-truths. Mostly I just apprehended that I was standing on the verge of a mystery—Baptism into Christ's death—about to take an action I couldn't even begin to comprehend until I'd already done it. That's inherently frightening. I didn't know what my future would look like, and I was aware that I wouldn't really be able to make competent guesses.

On Holy Saturday we had a rehearsal where we went through everything we'd have to do to receive Baptism and Confirmation. I pushed past everyone else to get out of the church as fast as possible so I could throw up. That weekend was one of only a handful of times in my life when I've managed to make myself physically ill from stress.

But those sessions during the Triduum were immensely helpful for me. What steadied me wasn't St. Edith's phenomenology but the eucharistic adoration itself. I knelt in front of the Body and Blood of Christ and felt grounded. I felt that I was, finally, at home; I was in my place.

There were many elements of this feeling. Kneeling in prayer is a way of speaking to God when you don't know what to say. You're speaking with your body, taking on a position of humility. Offering myself to God like that felt completely right.

I also felt intensely aware of the physical world. God himself had come into this world and experienced life in the flesh, and he came to us constantly, eternally entering into the temporal world in the bread and wine. The world we felt under our fingertips had been not only created in love and sustained through love but also exalted through the Incarnation. After being broken on the cross, after suffering the terrible wounds of love, Christ returns to us in the transformation of the wine and wafer. There were no words here I needed to struggle to understand, no theology to garble as I tried to explain my conversion to others. There was just the Word, vulnerable and humble in the Eucharist: Like the carol "What Child Is This?"

> *Good Christians, fear, for sinners here*
> *The silent Word is pleading.*[4]

During my Baptism and Confirmation, I was very distracted. I only remember two things about it: I forgot to return the towel they gave us to wipe off the excess holy oils; and my best friend, Meredith, who was an atheist, came to see it even though she'd said that she wouldn't. It took me years to tell her how much that gesture meant to me. I was under no illusions that she suddenly agreed with me or that she thought the Catholic Church was anything other than a mistaken and often abusive cadre with some nice paintings, but I understood her gesture as one of support for me as a person. She was willing to walk alongside me even into the belly of the beast. (This understanding of what it means to attend an event whose meaning you strongly disagree with has shaped my sense of how to respond to friends' gay marriages. I've written more about that subject in appendix two.)

Afterward there was a party, and we ate meat! And I promptly went about the business of sullying my newborn soul. I think I went about a week before I needed my first confession.

chapter four
Lather, Rinse, Repent

Looking back, what's most striking to me about my conversion is how little I knew what I was doing. As I said earlier, I didn't know *any* other queer Catholics who attempted to practice their faith. I didn't even know *of* any such people. (I hadn't yet read much about Oscar Wilde's long-term, sordid love affair with the Church in whose embrace he died.) I was sunnily convinced that I could do it, even though I knew of nobody else who ever had.

More troublingly, my approach to sin and virtue was summarized by the question, "How far can you go?" And I don't mean, "How far can you go toward sanctity?" I slept in bed with my boyfriend and thought that was fine because I would elbow him away if he tried to get a hand up my blouse. I drank with rigor. (I probably shouldn't be proud of winning a drinking contest, largely through psychological intimidation, but I am. We played a *Star Wars*–based drinking game, and my team won before Luke even got off Tatooine.) I was catty, I loved to gossip, and I felt no qualms about insulting or mocking my opponents if I thought I was being funny.

Many years later, a friend whom I hadn't seen in a while considered me tipsily and pronounced, "You know, you're a much nicer person now. *Much* nicer." *Ah,* I thought, *this is one of those backhanded compliments I've been hearing about!*

There were certain things I knew you were supposed to confess, such as lying. I figured if I threw up, had a super-intense hangover, or had a "real" blackout—not just some kind of blur of tattered memories whirling in a broken zoetrope—then that meant I had been *too* drunk and should go to confession. I lied to myself a lot, and I told myself that the stupid, cruel, or embarrassing things I had done while drunk had little to do with the alcohol per se. I began to experience a phenomenon with which I would later become depressingly familiar, where my moral boundaries stretched far beyond what I once would have considered acceptable. If you had told me about some of the things I was doing, and the things that were happening to me, a year or so earlier I would have considered them signs of a serious alcohol problem, but now I accepted them more or less as normal. Both my morals and my sense of identity had become way too elastic, like the face of that plastic-surgery woman in the movie *Brazil*.

Of course, part of the problem was that drinking wasn't all bad, at that time. Liquor and drunkenness genuinely served to make me more social, helped me get over my intense fears of public speaking or presenting controversial opinions to people I admired, and helped forge some of my deepest and most lasting friendships. I have a lot of good stories about drunken adventures.

A couple friends have wondered how I view heavy collegiate drinking now, given that it not only turned into such a huge problem for me later but also could be seen to be a problem at the time. As of right now, I basically think this: Drinking can open a door in the mind and allow access to ideas we're too stable, careful, or self-respecting to entertain sober; and many of these ideas still bear fruit once the hangover has worn off. Under the influence, I was willing to sign my name to much more extreme statements. Some of those statements were dumb—I don't actually think, as I once argued during freshman year, that Haiti should form a military alliance with the District of Columbia. But those long nights when I carjacked my mind and took her for a joyride are also the nights when I first began to understand many illiberal ideas about the limits of rationality, the virtues of humiliation, and the need for an eros that begins in love of the other rather than love of the self. Those ideas have shaped my Christian life, even though their origin was not exactly in "the wine of resurrection" but rather the vodka of bad decisions. I like Herodotus' tale of the Persians who purportedly debated every political question twice: once drunk, once sober.

And most people are able to get the good out of epic drinking and, when the bad becomes too much, just stop. Almost all of my friends tapered off their drinking after graduation and are now respectable glass-of-wine types. You'd never guess that I once had to roll them off a baseball diamond in a cloud of gin fumes. The friendships we forged during the sloshy years remain. When I was in college, and for a while after, liquor did exactly what it was supposed to do. It's just that it did other things too.

I've spent a lot of time on alcohol here, but there were many other areas where I was unconscious of any serious spiritual problem. I didn't realize how thoughtless and hurtful I could be. I was extremely sensitive to teasing, and yet teased other people; in many ways I "could dish it out, but couldn't take it," which is unpleasant to be around and humiliating to be. The biggest thing is that I wish I had thought of my spiritual life less as a game with rules, where the goal was avoidance of the kind of sin you definitely have to confess. I wish I'd thought of it more as an imitation of Christ, an attempt to build a civilization of love, or any more positive and Christ-centered understanding.

And I wish I'd thought of my role as a queer Catholic differently. For a long time I thought I had two projects when it came to the intersection of homosexuality and Christianity: an intellectual project, which meant learning about and attempting to understand the reasons behind the Church's teachings, and a negative, sin-avoidance project, which meant not having sex with girls.

Over time, my understanding of what I was supposed to be doing as a queer Catholic changed radically. I began to see that the intellectual project was interesting and necessary, but I was probably not the right person to do it; I lack the patience and academic temperament to do more than throw out suggestions, criticisms, and provocations. Its importance receded for me. Now and then I still read books about the "theology of the body" and so on, but I no longer think that a major part of my work as a queer Catholic is illuminating the philosophical and theological underpinnings of the Church's teaching on homosexuality.

Meanwhile the negative project of sin avoidance was replaced by a positive project of discerning my vocations. I began—slowly and painfully—to sense the gaps in my spiritual life and also to notice ways I'd found to partially fill them. Christian faith requires us to pour ourselves out like oil over the feet of our beloveds—the feet of Christ himself and of those around us. More or less by instinct, by feel, I had begun to discern what I got from loving women and how I could get some of those things without sinning against chastity. Through my friendships and my work at a crisis pregnancy center, I started to consider *how* and *whom* God was calling me to love.

*		*		*		*

While the changes I experienced in college were dramatic and fairly swift, the changes *after* college were deeper and slower. My life and self-concept after graduation in 2000 looked *very* different from my life and self-concept in 1996, but my 2002 self wouldn't appear radically different from my 2010 self, even though significant changes had gradually happened beneath the surface. I won't say those later changes were *more* important; they were necessary, but they wouldn't have happened without the initial catalyzing shock of conversion. However, many people criticize classic novels and movies for ending with the marriage of the heroes, when it's the long years after the marriage that are the toughest and, for that reason, most spiritually complex. We are better at writing romances than marriages (and better at writing adultery novels than marriage novels), and the same seems to hold true for conversion narratives. The leap of faith is easier to present in dramatic and compelling terms than the long climb up from wherever you've leapt *to*.

One commonplace in the recovery community is the idea that addicts get stalled at the age when we started using our drug of choice. So if you started drinking at age thirteen and have been sober for three years, your emotional or spiritual development is better analogized to a gawky, crazy adolescent than the forty-two-year-old your birth certificate documents. I think there are some ways this idea is true of me—being dishonest with myself and my confessors about the depth and intensity of my drinking problem did seriously stall my spiritual progress in all other areas of my life. But one weirdness of that post college, pre-sobriety stretch of time is that I really was deepening my faith in many ways, even as I also had this huge, monster pet sin crouching on my shoulder and weighing me down. My spiritual life was disjointed, compartmentalized. I learned a *lot* about apologizing and forgiving. I became, as my tipsy friend noted, a much less casually cruel person. It was easier for me to notice when I was being arrogant or judgmental. I even got better at controlling my temper, which has always been a major besetting sin of mine. I was pretty pleased with myself when a young woman who had known me for several years was startled when I said I had an awful temper: "I would never have thought that about you!" she said. "If anything, you seem very calm." This represented major progress for me.

All of these slow, small shifts helped me to acknowledge and address my alcoholism before it had taken too much away from me. The dishonesty, fear, and despair that characterized especially the later years of my drinking were obviously completely opposed to my faith and represented a huge chasm between my professed beliefs and my real-life actions. But as La Rochefoucauld said, "Hypocrisy is the tribute vice pays to virtue."[1] I was deeply hypocritical about my drinking. And yet I knew where virtue lay. Being Catholic provided me with both intense pressure to acknowledge my problem and the support I needed when I was finally able to try.

There were times when I was painfully aware of the fact that I was trying to help others live out their faith while letting myself slide further into addiction. It was a profoundly alienating feeling. I remember going to an early morning talk I was giving about crisis pregnancy counseling—I don't think I was actually hungover, but for some reason I was more intensely aware than usual of the fact that my drinking was out of control. A line from Nirvana's "Pennyroyal Tea" (an especially on-the-nose song in that situation) kept running through my head: *I'm a liar and a thief.*[2]

And yet I think the presentation was good. I did good work during those years, no matter what else was going on with me. But the work was not as good as it could have been, and living in that physician-heal-thyself state of mind is excruciating. Everything in your life starts to feel fake.

My memories of drinking in those years are so strange to me now. It seems obvious to me that I had a serious problem, and there were times when I tried to address that problem, mostly spurred by how much I hated needing to confess the same sins to the same priests. One priest told me (I still think wrongly) that I absolutely had to go to AA every day for a week. So I went, hungover, morbidly swilling coffee. Eventually a guy very kindly told me that if I wasn't serious there was no point in my being there. Another priest suggested that I try inpatient rehab. I tried all of the different tricks with which alcoholics are familiar: switching what I drank, making rules about *when* I could drink, *trying really hard this time*. The end result of all of that is that I mostly stopped getting drunk in public. At home, by myself, was very much another story.

How can someone live through these things and still compartmentalize to the degree that I did? My life seemed to me like two separate, hinged panels, and most of the time I kept them folded so the alcoholic panel was hidden.

Meanwhile, my imagination was narrowing. It became harder and harder for me to even conceive of a life without alcohol. I could give it up for Lent, sure (except when I couldn't, and with the caveat that Sundays weren't part of Lent). But forever?

The slow, seeping conviction that I needed to do *something* took a long time to turn into definite action. Some of it was that I was starting to lose what in AA jargon are called *yets*. These are the things that make us think we don't have a serious problem because they've never happened to us, when in reality, they just haven't happened *yet*. So for a while I had never had hallucinations caused by drinking or by alcohol withdrawal. I had never been hospitalized due to alcohol use. The year before I quit drinking both of those things stopped being yets. Some of it was that it was much harder to get to the good part of drinking; it seemed like I'd just barely start to feel a buzz and then black out. Some of it was that I had broken several expensive pieces of electronic equipment by spilling wine (or horrifying things like vodka with chocolate milk) on them. My apartment, never a luxury suite, was starting to look too much like how I felt.

I began to notice that my response to beauty was changing. Ordinarily when I would walk outside and see fiery Japanese maples, or a gold-and-purple sunset, or tulip trees in bloom, I would feel a rush of joy and gratitude. My only thought would be *Thank you!*

But when I needed to go to confession I would think, *I'm sorry.* I began to feel judged by and unworthy of the beauty all around me. It began to feel like something I had to hide from, and the old joy and gratitude began to feel very far away.

It felt like any faith I'd had was being slowly and methodically replaced by dread and despair. I knew I had to stop drinking, and I knew I couldn't.

The biggest step I took toward change, I think, was simply beginning to tell myself a different story in a distanced and dissociated way. I began to ask questions like, "If you were a different person, how would that different person address a drinking problem?" This was less threatening than thinking about my own life. Alcoholism confines the imagination; my recovery began when I started, slowly, to stretch and exercise it.

One answer I came up with was that a different person would find a spiritual director. And then of course I admitted that *I* could do that. A friend of mine who was also gay and celibate had a good relationship with his own spiritual director, a local priest. His recommendation meant a lot to me, because the last thing I wanted was someone who would try to persuade me that the real problem was my sexual orientation, my self-identification as gay rather than "struggling with same-sex attraction," my Catholic faith, or my celibacy.

Beginning to see a spiritual director was in no way an instant solution. You may have heard the old joke,

Q: How many therapists does it take to change a light bulb?

    A: Only one—but the light bulb has to really want to change.

That's cute enough, and true, but incomplete. The light bulb not only has to *want* to change; it has to believe that it can. Building up that belief takes time. I was still drinking through the first several months of spiritual direction. (I actually tried to hide that I was drunk during one session with the priest—surely if I have a delightful Caprese salad, to fill my stomach and change the smell of my breath, no one will notice!—and was intensely hungover for another session.) But my spiritual director did three major things for me. One was that he got me to start keeping a journal. Man, I was so sarcastic about this journal. I thought of diary keeping as a melodramatic, teenage thing to do, largely because the last time I'd kept a diary I had been a melodramatic teenager. *Oh, I need to write in my *~*journal*~**, I'd think, mentally adding the stars and sparkles. But the journal was a written record of how pointless drinking had become for me, how awful I felt when I did it, and how much better my mind and life seemed to work when I could stop for a while, even a short while.

My spiritual director was also my regular confessor, which meant that I didn't have to go through the unbearable explanations each time I had to go to confession—he made it much less punishing for me to come to the sacrament of Reconciliation, which meant that I could receive the Eucharist much more often, which is the truest foundation of our hope.

And most of all, the simple fact that I had reached out to him, "admitted to God, to ourselves, and to another human being the exact nature of our wrongs" as it says in AA's fifth step,[3] imagined the first leap upward and then actually taken it—that gave me hope that I could take the next step forward, and the next.

I was keeping all of this a secret from everyone except Meredith and my confessor. Both of them were gently nudging me to tell others, especially my parents, but I was adamant that I wasn't going to do that. I didn't want to worry them. My resistance only began to break down when it became obvious that whatever I was doing wasn't working for more than a week or two at a time. Taking my spiritual director's other suggestions had done me some good, and when Meredith gets to the point of urging me toward something, she's almost always right. Maybe they were both right on this question as well.

I screwed my courage to the sticking place—or *somewhere* sticky, anyway. What I actually did was have a couple vodka-and-whatevers and email my mom to suggest that we have lunch. Only in sober retrospect did I realize that telling my mother I had a serious drinking problem was not something you should do in a kicky little cafe, but by that point, the die had been cast, and I had to go through with it. Although it was the kind of conversation you never want to have from either end, Meredith and my spiritual director were both right that it changed something in me, in my self-concept. I made a promise and that promise actually strengthened my will. A little while after that I began to tell other friends that I had quit drinking.

Since then there have been two major kinds of challenges in my spiritual life: drinking-related challenges and everything-else-related challenges.

As for drinking, I went through temptations, the old cruel mental whispers that failure was inevitable so why not do it now? I reread my journal, which provided some armor. I read a lot about addiction, which also helped enormously.

The nonalcoholic challenges have been frustrating for me because I think I had the vague idea that if I could just stop drinking everything else in my spiritual life would fall into place. It turns out that I still have a hot temper. I'm still made angry and frustrated by failure, trivial mistakes, or bad luck. I still have a hard time being fully present in prayer instead of gabbling through the Rosary. I still put off confession even though I've learned time and time again that I feel and act better when I'm receiving Communion regularly.

There are still times when these difficulties and deficits in my character feel overwhelming. There are still times when "I snapped at someone" becomes "I'm a horrible person and should just not talk or interact with people ever." But the difference is that when I was drinking, especially toward the end, ninety percent of the time I felt despair at the thought that I could never fully fix myself, and ten percent of the time I felt terror. Now, ninety percent of the time I feel like if I get back on the horse, go to confession, and attempt to surrender more thoroughly to Christ and to what God wants for me, I will be able to make some kind of progress and accept whatever he chooses to do. God heals some wounds; others, like the wounds of Jesus that were still vivid and open after his Resurrection, God glorifies. Ninety percent of the time I feel like with prayer and humility I can do my best to accept either possibility. Ten percent of the time I feel slightly crazy and miserable, and when that happens I try to reread my journal, take a nap, or watch some figure skating on YouTube, and as time passes, things get better.

For some people it will appear obvious why I'm talking about addiction and recovery in a book that is, supposedly, really about being gay, chaste, and Catholic. These people believe that homosexuality is correlated with—and therefore causes—depression, addiction, and the heartbreak of psoriasis. Some of the statistics purporting to show these terrible outcomes are manipulated. (Paul Cameron, whose work claiming that less than two percent of gay men survive to old age was frequently cited in the '90s, based his statistics on a bleakly hilarious comparison of obituaries in gay newspapers to obituaries in mainstream ones.[4]) The rest might well be effects of stigma and minority status. (Comparisons to ethnic minorities don't work here for many reasons, of which the most obvious is that most black children grow up in black families, but most gay children grow up in straight families.)

Still, I realize I may not be the very best poster child to make the case for gay mental health. All I can say is that I know a lot of queer people who are so healthy and normal, you could just puke. They are veritable pillars of bourgeois stability. Not how I've ever wanted to live, but not exactly the movie *Cruising* either.

For other people the connection will be obvious for a different reason. These people believe that a gay life faithful to the Church's teaching is a life without love. They would attribute my alcoholism to my religion and, specifically, my acceptance of celibacy. Here again I realize I'm the poster child for a poster nobody wants on their wall! But again, I do actually know many celibate queer people who are leading productive, caring, love-filled lives, who are not addicts and never have been. You'll meet some of them in the rest of this book.

So it might be tempting to argue that there is *no* connection between the gay-Catholic part of this book—the main attraction—and this weird alcoholism sideshow. Is this just two unrelated books stapled together? I don't think so. I think there are a few different kinds of connection.

First, the longing for *ekstasis*, for astonishing contact with something beyond and much greater than the self, did drive some of my drinking as well as some of my search for God. There were many other factors in both, but this thirst for rapture was part of it. Both Stephen King and (especially) Tim Powers have written novels that capture the almost erotic, or ersatz-erotic, longing for alcohol. (If you want to get a sense of what the bridal mysticism of the bottle looks like, I highly recommend Powers's *Last Call* and *The Stress of Her Regard*.) There's a reason scripture uses metaphors like "the wine of astonishment," while in Acts 2:13 some people overhearing Christ's disciples speaking in tongues at Pentecost thought that the disciples must be drunk. That rapture, which is briefly and damagingly fulfilled in drunkenness, is genuinely and lastingly fulfilled in Christ. The blood of Christ is more truly intoxicating than mere wine. And for at least some alcoholics—I think there are many kinds of addiction, and many of them are best addressed first with therapeutic and medical treatment rather than solely spiritual guidance—it is God who finally slakes the thirst.

The second connection is the small but real way in which the heartbreak-of-psoriasis school is sort of right. Being gay does present barriers to feeling like you belong. Alcohol, which lowers inhibitions and eases social situations, can lower those barriers. The problem is that for alcoholics, what at first helped us forge connections with other people and be vulnerable and honest with them eventually separates us and leads us to lies and self-deception.

The third link is that there *were* ways in which the structure of my celibate life (which isn't the structure of every celibate gay life) made both drinking and denial easier. This is the problem of lack of accountability.

It's easy to get defensive about this issue. Marriage isn't exactly a flawless protective shield against addiction, obviously. This is especially true for me because I tend to fall for other heavy drinkers, to whom marriage might even present extra risks. And there are ways of structuring a celibate life—by living in an intentional religious community, living with friends, or living with family, for example—in which you do have the constant check on your behavior of someone to come home to. While I was writing the first draft of this book, I lived with my parents for financial reasons. Although I'm glad that I didn't move back there until I had gained some experience in being sober while living on my own, it's certainly much easier to stay sober when you are living with people you love. I'm not going to pretend that celibacy is a way of life without its own specific temptations; the isolation, which allowed me to keep drinking so heavily for so long, is one major problem many celibate laypeople will face, regardless of orientation. (A friend of mine pointed out that the isolation in which I drank, at the end, could be analogized to its own kind of closet, with all the fear and shame the closet so often brings.) The rest of this book will, I hope, offer ways to create a celibate queer life that is better than the one I used to have.

But the fourth link between my drinking and my Catholicism is the one I'm most interested in right now, since it ties in with the major theme of this book. As I've said, when I first converted, I basically thought that chastity for a gay Catholic was purely a negative rule or outer boundary: don't have sex with girls. Over time I learned that you need to structure your life in such a way that you are living out a positive vocation to love. You are called *to* something, not merely away from something. And similarly, I don't think sobriety is the same as not drinking. I don't think my task is best understood as a negative one of avoiding drunkenness or avoiding alcohol. My project right now is to build a way of life in keeping with my God-given vocation. And thinking about sobriety in this way helps me to see that I need to be more connected to others: more honest with my friends, and therefore more intimate with them, and closer to my family. Not having gay sex and not drinking are things I can do on my own, at least for a while. Living out my vocation is something I can only do *with* the people I'm called to love.

chapter five

Three Kinds of
Diversity in Gay
Christian Lives

I've told you my story because I think it's natural to ask, "Where on earth did you come from to end up where you are now?"

But I also wanted to tell my own story precisely because it's only one story among others. Many of my gay, celibate friends had totally different experiences. There are at least three places where Christian writers—including me, I'm sorry to say—are often way too quick to assume that our own experiences and preferences are universal: whether there's an intelligible "origin story" for homosexuality (and whether investigating possible origins for one's own homosexuality is spiritually fruitful or harmful); which metaphors best describe gay Christians' condition and our spiritual needs; and what the role of sublimation is in celibate life.

What Is the Point of an Origin Story?

American Christianity seems obsessed with figuring out why people are gay, as if that would solve the moral, theological, or pastoral problems we face. I hope that the story I've told will illustrate how complex and multilayered our histories can be. This section will explore what you might learn from asking yourself, "Why am I gay?"—and what the spiritual dangers might be in letting that exploration become too important to you.

In 2006 I attended a conference of the ex-gay group Love Won Out. (I was on assignment for *National Review Online*; you can find my article, "Homo No Mo'?", on their website.) At the conference I heard a talk given by Joseph Nicolosi of the National Association for Research and Therapy of Homosexuality (NARTH), in which he described the "pre-homosexual" child. My childhood self fit his description pretty closely. I was "imaginative, theatrical, lonely, quick to internalize criticism."[1]

Oh, wait—that's the "pre-homosexual" *boy*. If I had grown up into a gay man, Nicolosi's description would ring fairly true! . . . Except, obviously, for the parts about feeling insecure in one's gender identity and having difficult relationships with one's parents. I enjoyed reasonably gender-normative '80s childhood activities, such as playing Cat-Ra to another girl's She-Ra or picking out which members of U2 would be our future husbands. (I think I got The Edge.) And I've always felt very loved and supported by my parents.

The "pre-homosexual" girl gets a lot less ink. Most of the theories about her focus on problems with attachment to the mother. At that same Love Won Out conference, Melissa Fryrear categorized the mothers of girls who became lesbians with a series of (sometimes conflicting) negative attributes: They were doormats, or they were domineering, or they were too concerned with being their children's "best friend" rather than a parent. These descriptions are more or less a photographic negative, everything my mom isn't—despite giving so many possible origins that you'd think some of them might have fit.

Lesbianism is also often attributed to sexual abuse. Fryrear actually said that she'd *never* met a lesbian who wasn't sexually abused. I wish I had gone up to her afterward and introduced myself, so she couldn't use that line anymore.

I don't want to claim that sexual abuse never shifts someone's sexual orientation, since sexuality is complex and responds to our circumstances, culture, and experiences. But someone can be both an abuse survivor and a lesbian without thinking the former caused the latter. As with every painful family dynamic or element of personal history identified by the ex-gay theories, it's entirely possible to experience real healing of the wounds of your past without experiencing any change in your orientation. It's possible to experience real healing without *desiring* any change in your orientation. While some people do believe that their homosexuality is connected in some way to family problems or abuse, many others view their painful pasts as separate from their sexual orientation. People with both of these perspectives pursue chastity. There just doesn't seem to be anything gained from lecturing people about the correct way to interpret the most painful events of their lives. I have never once seen someone benefit spiritually from being told to accept an "origin story" for their homosexuality that didn't ring true to them. Quite the opposite: I've very, very often seen people spiritually harmed by this insistence.

A friend added that in his experience the "origin stories" for homosexuality proposed by groups like NARTH tend to work like astrology. Sure, you might read the description of a Scorpio and say, "Oh, I totally do those things!", but that's because the descriptions are either extremely vague or offer so many possible personality traits and explanations that you're bound to fit at least some of them.

That said, I do believe there are people for whom the psychological "origin stories" are true. Certainly there are people for whom those stories resonate deeply. Because *homosexuality* is an umbrella term covering a lot of different styles of sexuality, and because people's childhoods and family dynamics clearly

do affect their later relationships and psychosexual development, it shouldn't be surprising to find that there are some family
dynamics that *may* predispose someone (especially when there's
also already a genetic predisposition) to homosexuality. We
don't actually know if that's true or not, but again, it shouldn't
be surprising, and it certainly shouldn't be threatening to gay
people. After all, saying that some kinds of homosexuality may
be caused in part by family dynamics doesn't imply that these
kinds of homosexuality are chosen or changeable—or somehow
less genuine.

So the bigger question isn't, "What is the origin of homosexuality?" or even, "What is the origin of *my* sexual orientation?"—
questions with many possible answers and no definite ones. The
bigger and better question is, "What can we gain from investigating the possible origins of our own sexualities?"

The answer to this question is even more complex than the
answer to the first ones. Many people will find that the answer is,
"Nothing." If you have no particular interest in the reasons you're
gay or none of the origin stories resonate with you, I don't think
there's any reason you should push yourself to find or imagine
some hidden psychological trauma. This quest for trauma dam-
ages relationships between parents and children—parents blame
themselves, children blame parents.

The blog *Disputed Mutability* is one of the best resources out
there if you're interested in ex-gay ministry and psychology. In
one post the pseudonymous blogger describes the severe consequences of her attempt to follow the psychological scripts given
by the ex-gay movement.

She wrote that "The theories became self-fulfilling prophe-
cies for me." She felt pressured to affirm that she was broken, a
"love-starved little child . . . on the inside," and so she began to
act accordingly.

Thus, when I was into these sorts of theories, I was very self-obsessed, very focused on my needs, in part because the ex-gay theology I accepted was very focused on my needs. I was told by ex-gay literature that my mission was to make sure I got my needs met and my relational deficits filled. So I became the taker (and not a giver) in my relationships with others, in large part because I believed I desperately needed to take, and I believed I had little to give.

Moreover, far from healing her familial relationships, the ex-gay scripts and origin stories actually damaged them:

The other way these theories worked as a self-fulfilling prophecy in my life is in my relationship with my parents. Anyone who has followed my story at all will note that my relationship with my parents was sub-optimal. There is no use denying that. But I will say that spending years trying to diagnose what they did and how it might have caused my homosexual issues made our relationship worse rather than better. It increased the distance between me and my mom rather than diminishing it. It led me to turn my frustration with my same-sex attracted predicament (and it certainly felt like a predicament at times!) toward them. Every time I saw a fault in my mother or father, I would make a mental note of it, and remember how they did something vaguely similar when I was little, and how that probably contributed to my struggle in some way. Often I felt rather bitter about it, especially when I was having a tough time of things. And that drove a wedge into our already flawed relationship.

Please don't get me wrong—the ex-gay movement does *not* endorse either of these things. They do not approve of behaving selfishly and immaturely, or of feeling bitter toward one's parents. But in spite of their explicit stance, I found both of those problems to be very real side effects of these theories, potential pitfalls that I stumbled into. I accept responsibility for that, but the role these theories played in my choices is not negligible.

There's more. *Disputed Mutability* wrote:

> I once had a series of conversations with an ex-gay where the pressure to come up with a sexual abuse history was pretty overwhelming. I had no recollection of sexual abuse, but she kept bringing up the possibility. Weren't there, after all, periods of time in my childhood that I couldn't remember? (Well yeah, but does any adult completely remember their entire childhood? Isn't it all bits and pieces for most of us?) Wasn't it *possible* that I was abused during those times, and simply blocked out the trauma? With gentle coaching of this other ex-gay, I made the leap from "possible" to "probable" to "almost certain" in about ten seconds flat.
>
> Later, I was informed by an ex-gay leader that one hundred percent of people with a set of issues like mine were victims of sexual abuse. One hundred percent. Unequivocally, totally confident, without a doubt. I walked away from that conversation rather dazed. I had no knowledge of ever having been sexually abused, but now it seemed like it had to be so.

And after all of that pain, all of the familial conflict and depleted integrity caused by *Disputed Mutability's* desire to accept the ex-gay psychological model and be healed of her homosexuality . . . she was just as gay when she finally ditched this approach as she had been when she started. Later, after she had begun to view her sexual temptations as just another form of sin rather than a sign of major psychological damage, she did fall in love with a man and is now married with kids—which makes her blunt rejection of the ex-gay "origin story" all the more powerful.[2]

My strongest suggestion is that "origin stories" for homosexuality typically identify psychological wounds and spiritual needs. If you find those stories resonant and reflective of your own experience or emotions, then you should seek healing for those psychological wounds or fulfillment of those spiritual needs, *because they're wounds and needs*. Not because they contributed to the development of your homosexuality. I do know some men who have experienced healing and spiritual growth by working on their relationships with their fathers or finding nonsexual ways to meet their need for intimacy and warmth from men. By working on honesty and forgiveness in their families of origin or developing strong friendships with men, they've healed a lot of the wounds that made the psychological origin stories of homosexuality resonate with them.

Some of these friends found that this healing corresponded with a diminishing of homosexual feelings and an increasing of heterosexual feelings. (Those obviously aren't the same thing. You can go from having a lot of urgent homosexual desire to having not very much sexual desire of any kind.) Other friends found that they were still, you know, super gay.

Both groups of men were really glad they'd sought help: sometimes from therapists or spiritual directors and always from friends. Both groups of men made great spiritual progress. And the degree to which they progressed seemed completely distinct from whether their sexual orientation shifted.

In healing childhood or adolescent hurts, they found a lot of peace. In pursuing understanding, forgiveness, or friendship, they grew closer to other people—and closer to being the person God wanted them to be, closer to being a saint. But our job is to be the kind of saint God is calling us to be, not the kind of saint we want to be, or the kind of saint our parents might want us to be.

If the quest for an explanation distracts you from that goal, it is leading you away from God. It would be a terrible tragedy to pursue orientation change because you think God demands it of you, only to end up straight but unforgiving, closed off from intimacy with others, spiritually proud, or otherwise distant from God and from those around you.

Your Love Is Like Bad Metaphors

People sometimes refer to me as "struggling with same-sex attraction." That language ignores the fact that I *don't* particularly struggle with my orientation. (I struggle a lot more with resentment toward well-meaning straight Christians who assume that I struggle with it.) And, more importantly than that, I find that it's much easier for me to follow Christ when I think of myself as surrendering to him in all of the places where I'm tempted. Picturing myself as "struggling" with temptations of any kind makes me feel like I'm relying on my own strength and competence. "Struggling" sounds like the exact kind of physical task I'm terrible at! It's as if I'm being told that in order to love Jesus, I need to get good at softball. This will never happen.

Many people have other problems with the language of "struggling with same-sex attraction." For them, this language separates out a part of themselves and animates it, making it into a kind of living enemy, which plays into a lot of self-hatred and makes them feel internally divided rather than united in love of Christ.

For other people, this same language of internal division captures how they feel. They like the ability to think of their same-sex attraction as a consequence of the fall of man, not something inherent in their makeup. They think of it as something they can *offer* to God precisely because it isn't an inseparable part of their nature.

I love metaphors of surrender and submission. They capture how I feel when I'm acting well and serving God. They offer reassurance that I'm not relying on my own strength but on Christ's sacrifice. I'm being carried by the Lord—"leaning on the everlasting arms," as the hymn says.

But for other people, language of surrender and submission seems as if it's requiring them to give up their personalities. That language feels passive to them, and therefore is despairing. It can even feel like a counsel of political quietism: spend so much time focusing on your own *surrender* that you never get around to making life better for others, changing the culture, challenging assumptions, or fighting against the abuse and isolation of queer kids.

Recovery Options: The Complete Guide by Joseph Volpicelli and Maia Szalavitz (a terrific book in its own right, and if you're dealing with addiction in your own life or that of someone you love, I highly recommend it) captures these problems with "surrender" language as used in Alcoholics Anonymous and other twelve-step groups:

> Women for Sobriety (WFS) was founded in 1976, when Jean Kirkpatrick (not the former U.N. Ambassador) recognized that many of the principles of AA did not meet women's needs. As an alcoholic herself, she struggled with AA's ideology. She noted that the steps particularly focused on encouraging humility and recognition of one's flaws. However, most female alcoholics already spend too much time on these problems—hating themselves because they aren't living up to what they think a woman should be. Their main issue is often not to become less arrogant and more responsive to the needs of others, but to feel better about themselves and to take their own needs into account in their lives.[3]

Of course, not all women will agree. The "surrender" language expresses what I both need and want. I have a lot of the self-aggrandizing qualities and the corresponding need for humility for which AA's language was designed. And, maybe because I heard way too much jargon in elementary and middle school, I tend to be skeptical of anything trying to boost my self-esteem.

But my point is that not everyone has the same spiritual needs I have, and therefore not everyone will be helped by the language, metaphors, and corresponding self-understandings that have helped me. Therefore, when people reject one metaphor for their lives—whether the metaphor is being used to understand their sexuality, their addiction, or anything else—they shouldn't be dismissed as in denial or resisting help. They may be expressing a genuine insight into their own spiritual needs and their own path to God.

One Christian alternative to the language of surrender might be the language of liberation. Christ sets us free—from slavery to sin, from fear of others' judgments, from conformity, from despair. "For freedom Christ set us free; so stand firm, and do not submit again to the yoke of slavery" (Gal 5:1). This is language for people who need liberation not only from sin but from oppression. Christ as Liberator rejects the sinful hierarchies that place men above women, rich above poor, married above unmarried, and straight above gay. Christ comes to transform both our individual hearts and our societies.

Wesley Hill's excellent book *Washed and Waiting: Reflections on Christian Faithfulness and Homosexuality* uses two different metaphors in its title. There's the metaphor of washing, which gives a picture of God's tender parental care and the way he prepares us to go out and act in the world, "cleansed and conformed unto Thy will."[4] But the second word, "waiting," is also a metaphor: suspense, the not-yet, an active longing for the Lord and attention to the fact that this world is always passing away. "Washed and waiting" is a state of readiness for action *and* a state of patience. Inherent in the book's title is the fact that one way of understanding your life as a gay Christian may not be enough: You may need multiple perspectives, multiple ways of talking about what you need to do, multiple metaphors.

Sublimation Takes Coordination

The concept of sublimation begins with the idea that there are several different types of love; a classical division includes *agape, storge, eros,* and *philia.* An intense desire or longing for another person or for a relationship may not have taken one of these specific forms yet. We may yearn for another person, or even for something less formed like "service to women," without that yearning taking on an erotic character or suggesting anything sexual. And so this longing can be directed away from eros, and away from sex (a separate question), and toward friendship or charity.

Moreover, even when the longing has already taken on a specifically erotic character, it can be transformed from one type of love into another. Many of us have experienced at least one friendship that began with an erotic charge but now has basically no eros and only philia. The love hasn't diminished, and in fact has typically deepened with time, but its character has shifted. The urgency, neediness, and *lack* aren't a part of the friendship's motivating force anymore. The friendship has often developed a greater equality (rather than the interplay of lover and beloved), a greater similarity (rather than the erotic charge of difference), and a greater security and comfort.

Sublimation can be used to describe this shift from eros to another form of love. But perhaps the most important point about sublimation is that it can also be a way to express eros in actions other than the obvious ones. For example, eros can be expressed in artistic creation or philosophy rather than in sex.

This is why it's possible to talk about something like "the erotics of teaching"—not because teachers want to sleep with their students, but because the teacher-student relationship often has elements of the kind of neediness, the yearning to fill a void in someone's soul or to be filled, the recognition of oneself in someone quite different, and other features that are part of the electrical charge of eros. Sleeping with your student turns out to be a great way to learn that sex *isn't* what the erotics of the teaching relationship were actually directed toward; sex does a far worse job of fulfilling those erotic needs than, say, mentoring the student until she can take on leadership and teaching positions of her own.

For a Christian, all love ultimately has its source in God, and the love between God and man is the template for love between humans. And in both the Hebrew Bible and the New Testament, divine love presents itself in erotic imagery because it has erotic characteristics. Reverse engineering this process may give some ideas of how to sublimate one's eros into love of God.

Another way to think about sublimation might be to think of the soul as a kaleidoscope. We're filled with a wide array of needs and longings, each one with several sparkling facets. Turn the kaleidoscope one way and these longings arrange themselves into a pattern our culture has decided to call "lesbianism." But we may find other ways to turn the kaleidoscope so that some of the pieces—perhaps the longings to be touched, to be known, to be of service, to be family—form other patterns in which our longings can be fulfilled in other ways. These new patterns won't include every single stone from the "lesbian" array, but they will be beautiful in their own right. Asking ourselves what our necklaces and spirals of longing are made up of, which stones compose them, may help us see that many of those glinting pieces can become part of different patterns such as friendship or solidarity.

But I'm better at pointing at examples of sublimation than at telling you how it works or how you might do it. I can't write a how-to guide. And many people find the concept of sublimation of eros kind of blankly unintelligible: they acknowledge that other people seem to do it and to get a lot out of it, but for them, it doesn't make sense. I think I'm unusually attuned to sublimation, whether to performing it or simply to noticing its presence, but it's totally OK if you just don't care about this subject.

As same-sex attracted Christians, we can ask two questions: "How am I being called to love and be loved?" *and* "What can I do with my sexual desires that would serve God?" Sublimation *only* answers the second question—and it's only one possible answer. I tend to think in terms of how I can express my desire for women in ways that are beautiful and pleasing to God. Others will think in terms of how they can sacrifice their same-sex erotic desire, nail it to the Cross or pour it out like oil over the feet of the Beloved, and that is perhaps an even more sublime and poignant way of serving God through our desires. It's probably a harder way, but if sacrifice rather than expression is the road you're called to walk, there's no point in avoiding it.

In writing about vocation, I hope to answer the first and most important question: to help celibate gay Christians find ways of loving and being loved. That will make your life immensely richer and more pleasing to God, even if you still feel like you don't know what to do with your same-sex attractions or what the point of them even is. Even if you feel like all you can do with your erotic attractions is deny them what they want, you don't have to deny *yourself* love.

part two

You Are Called to Love

chapter six
What Vocation Is and Is Not

It is still true that in over thirty years of weekly churchgoing, I have never heard a homily that attempted to explain how a gay man should live, or how his sexuality should be expressed. I have heard nothing but a vast and endless and embarrassed silence, an awkward, unexpressed desire for the simple nonexistence of such people, for their absence from the moral and physical universe, for a word or a phrase, like "objective disorder," that could simply abolish the problem they represented and the diverse humanity they symbolized. The teaching I inherited was a teaching that, in the best of all possible worlds, I simply would not exist. And it was hard to disobey this; since it was not an order, it was merely a wish.

If articulated, I suppose, the order was abstinence. Abstinence forever; abstinence always; abstinence not for the sake of something else, but for its own sake; abstinence not just from sex, but from love and love's hope and the touch of a lover's embrace. Abstinence even from recognition, acknowledgment, family.

—Andrew Sullivan
Love Undetectable: Notes on Friendship, Sex and Survival,
pages 42–43

Last Sunday we had a priest give a special announcement at the end of Mass, urging us all to sign up for the Run for Vocations.

This is the way we typically hear the term used in the Catholic Church today, if we hear it at all: *Vocation* means call to the ordained priesthood, with maybe a little asterisk suggesting you could also be a friar, a deacon, or a religious sister.

Based on this model of discerning a vocation to the priesthood, Catholics sometimes talk about "the vocation of marriage" or even—and I think this is a mistake, though many Catholics I respect disagree—"the vocation of singleness."

The way I'm using the term in this book is different. In my view everyone has a vocation, and probably more than one. A vocation is the path or way of life in which God is calling us to pour out our love for him and for other particular human beings. Vocation is always a positive act of love, not a refraining-from-action. So celibacy, in and of itself, isn't a vocation in this sense, although it can be a discipline that frees one up for one's vocations. Singleness is *especially* not a vocation in this sense, since singleness is defined by lack of connection to others.

By this definition of vocation, there can never be an exhaustive list of all the possible vocations. That's fine by me, since some vocations seem to emerge in the course of Christian history and then fade, like the Russian Orthodox *yurodivy* or holy fool. Vocations reemerge, shift, and change. Today's *intentional communities* don't look much like thirteenth-century *beguinages*, but they're both attempts to form communities of laypeople living in service to Christ. The vowed, familial same-sex friendships depicted in Alan Bray's beautiful historical study *The Friend* (discussed much more later) have almost entirely disappeared, and if the practice were to be revived, it would necessarily carry a somewhat different meaning and face vastly different challenges.

In this understanding the priesthood definitely is a vocation—and there may also be a more specific vocation, such as a call to be a Franciscan or a Jesuit. Other forms of religious life also fit the model. So does marriage. But so does being a daughter, if that role is one of the primary ways in which you give yourself to others in love. You may have a vocation to friendship, to ministry in prisons, to artistic creation. Here are a few general statements that apply to all of our vocations.

Vocation Is Only Partly Chosen

"Well, of course I think celibacy is fine for people who have a call to that, like priests, but I don't think every gay person is called to celibacy." This is a statement I hear often, and it does open up some necessary questions. I'll start by explaining why I don't think this is a good model of how vocation to the priest-hood works because I think that will help us enter into a broader discussion of the complex interaction of unchosen and chosen sacrifices in Christian life.

Some priests do find the concept of celibacy attractive. The discipline makes them available to others in a radical way; it frees them from responsibilities for a wife and children in order to make them all the more responsible for an entire flock. But many priests discern a vocation to the priesthood *without* a simul-taneously discerned call to celibacy, or a sense that the celibate life is unusually fitting for them. They don't actually feel any particular call to be "eunuchs for the kingdom of heaven." That discipline comes to them as a consequence of other facts, such as their call to be a priest in the Western church. This separation of discerning a call to priesthood versus accepting a discipline of celibacy shouldn't be too surprising, since celibacy is not a uni-versal requirement for the priesthood even in the Western church (where exceptions are made for, among others, married priests leaving Anglican orders for Catholic ones) and has never been a requirement for priesthood in the East, whether in Orthodox Christianity or in Eastern Rite Catholicism.

For many of us, our vocations work this way too. We discern the call, but it comes with consequences, and we have to work to accept those consequences even when we don't feel drawn to them in any way. This is true of almost all vocations. I think we've all known parents who long for children and sacrifice deeply and instinctively for their kids, but have a hard time sacrificing their *self-image* or the future they imagined for their children. They sacrifice time, money, and emotional resources and spend endless hours teaching, comforting, disciplining and cuddling, but they find it almost impossible to do one of the biggest tasks of parenthood—letting go.

This is, I think, one of the biggest truths about all vocations, not just gay people's vocations: the sacrifice God wants isn't always the sacrifice you wanted to make. And when you know how ready you are to sacrifice a great deal, *as long as you get to do it on your terms*, it can feel especially painful and unfair when God asks you for something different, a sacrifice you never wanted. Good gay relationships are often sacrificial. They are loyal, vulnerable, forms of loving service, and a school for humility and forgiveness. But they aren't the sacrifice God is calling you to make.

Some vocations do present themselves mostly as a choice. A woman may discern a call to be a religious sister, but find that God has left the choice between two religious orders more or less up to her. But very often God leaves us only one choice—yes or no?

Even if I did have a specific desire for celibacy, by the way, that wouldn't imply a particular vocation. People often ask me, "Why don't you just become a nun?" as if the definition of a *nun* is a Catholic woman who doesn't have sex. Have these people met me? I would be a terrible nun! I lack patience, I am not good at getting used to new people, and I have issues with authority. Nobody wants to deal with a bohemian nun.

More seriously, a vocation to vowed religious life is a *specific* calling I don't have. It isn't, or shouldn't be, a scrap basket for all the girls who aren't planning to get married. As women's secular opportunities expanded and "taking the veil" was no longer one of the only alternatives to marriage available for women, we should have become much more aware of the specific beauties and challenges of women's religious life. We should have become more aware of vowed religious life as a call from God, rather than a *faute de mieux* kludge for a sexist culture. If we take women's religious calling seriously as a call from God rather than the solution to a cultural problem, we won't ask (sincerely or flippantly) why every same-sex attracted celibate woman doesn't just nun up.

Every Vocation Has a Cross as Well as a Crown

I spoke about sacrifice previously because every vocation eventually requires it. If you take vows of chastity, obedience, and poverty, those sacrifices may seem more obvious; but all vocations can be, at times, a cross to bear.

Specifically, every vocation has its own form of loneliness. I think of two things when I consider this question. The first is a scene from David Lodge's 1982 novel, *How Far Can You Go?* in which a group of young Catholics confront a confusing and painful post–Vatican II world. In this scene a gay Catholic and a straight married man somewhat waspishly talk past each other, avoiding the subject of their respective struggles. The gay man condescendingly defends the Church's opposition to birth control, and the married man, silently but equally condescendingly, thinks, *It's all very well for you.* Neither of them is able to break out of the plastic bubble of his own suffering long enough to listen to and love the other.

The second thought is something an English professor at Yale said one day during a lecture on Coleridge. This man—who, by the way, was married—interrupted his discourse on "The Rime of the Ancient Mariner," glared bleakly out into space above the heads of the students, and said that the poem was really about "how you can be more alone . . . when you're with somebody else . . . than when you're all by yourself."[1] Having given the students this insight into the nature of marriage (and friendship!), he returned to his albatross.

But just as marriage and friendship carry their own forms of loneliness, so vocations that appear more painful may carry their own joys—if you let them. One theme of this book is that celibacy is not enough for gay people and that we must cultivate an outward looking spirituality, which seeks to love and serve others. It's OK to get "bachelor weird" if you live alone, but don't get stuck in your rut, turned in on yourself and isolated. That will not only keep you from supporting others and therefore make their lives more difficult, it'll make your own life more difficult too, since you will miss out on some of the joys that are offered to you in a celibate lay life.

You may have more freedom, including more freedom to serve. When I was living by myself, I was able to occasionally give shelter to homeless women, which I can't do now that I'm living with my parents. This was a blessing to *me*, not just to them. A celibate lay life also allows more free time to refocus myself, get centered, and give my time and my attention entirely to God. This intimate, one-on-one time with the Lord, when you're not exhausted and distracted, is something many parents miss. It's a privilege, and one for which I'm grateful.

My point is not that all vocations are the same. I'm not trying to say, "Stop whining. Married people suffer, too!"

Nor do I agree with people who argue that straight single people are in "the same situation" as gay people, since they too must be celibate. That formulation ignores the ways in which being straight and unmarried may be *harder*—for example, I don't have to wonder and worry about why I haven't found the right man or why I'm not coupled up like my friends.

And it also ignores the unique challenges and humiliations of being a gay Christian: coming out (and deciding whether to come out), dealing with parental rejection, being a political football and a symbol of whatever everybody doesn't like about the Church, trying to understand and cope with Church *pronunciamentos* and directives, being targeted for violence and discrimination, and, perhaps most of all, having achingly few models for your way of life. Not to mention, of course, knowing that unless something major and really weird happens to you, your current difficult, hard-to-explain situation, which receives literally *no* representation in mainstream culture, will last the rest of your life.

I don't think all Christians are similarly situated. I don't think our crosses and our joys are the same. But I do think we can learn from one another if we're willing to listen. Keeping in mind that every vocation has specific forms of sacrifice and loneliness associated with it can help us avoid envy and despair. We can look for ways of learning from the experiences of others (even people quite different from ourselves) and get realistic preparation for our vocations rather than fluffy happily-ever-after dreams.

You Learn to Live Out Your Vocation by Loving

I've stitched together a weird, patchwork vocation for myself. I did it through intuition and the time-honored method of throwing spaghetti at the wall to see if it sticks. I didn't actually sit down and read books on how to find my vocation, although I certainly hope such a book would have had some value since I appear to be writing one.

Sometimes I more or less woke up and found myself already within a vocation. Many of my closest friendships are relationships that seemed to happen to me rather than being chosen by me. I needed only to recognize these friendships as ways in which God was calling me to love others, and then live out that love to the best of my ability. I worked on maintaining these friendships through the usual practices of self-giving, being present to the other person, apologizing when you've done wrong, and forgiving when wrong has been done to you. In turn the friendships made me, I think, a gentler person.

Other times I felt a lack and sought ways to fill it, as with the pregnancy center work. The center has four major functions: We provide direct material help for pregnant women and families with young kids (so we give out diapers, wipes, formula, clothes, strollers, car seats, and many other items). We do free pregnancy testing. We try to connect women with other services and community groups or sources of support. (We run our own childbirth and parenting classes, for example, but also help low-income women find rental assistance programs, mental health care, shelters, and other places that can fill the needs we can't address ourselves.) And we do counseling on pretty much anything a client might be dealing with. It is a pro-life center, but I've been surprised at how holistic the work ends up being—which is appropriate since it is also, centrally, a Christian ministry.[2]

My evenings at the pregnancy center are basically unpredictable. Some days I mostly just coo at cute kids and bag up diapers and clothes. Other days I'll spend an hour with a woman struggling to leave an abusive boyfriend and then another hour with a frightened girl whose mother is pressuring her into an abortion. The fact that the work is so emotionally intense and so woman-centered makes me imagine that I now know what '70s feminist "consciousness-raising" groups might have felt like, even though I doubt many of those groups would approve of pro-life Christian counseling. But there's the same need to work *with* the client, to strengthen her and support her, and listen for the places where she's ready to take a step forward in her life, and encourage her there.

This work has many traits in common with the work of friendship. It's incredibly rewarding—the pregnancy center has been a place of great solace for me even when my spiritual life was at its most chaotic. It's humbling and requires a deep acceptance that you cannot live someone else's life for her, you can't say or do the perfect thing, and you have to love people who are doing things you believe to be both morally wrong and self-damaging. The client doesn't need *you*, but she needs the love and forgiveness that can flow through you. And then she needs you to let her go and not invest your own ego in convincing her to do the right thing.

It's a surprisingly mutual relationship. I've been guided as much by clients as I've guided them, if not more. And the more effort you put into letting the relationship be reciprocal rather than hierarchical, the more vulnerable you make yourself and the richer the relationship becomes.

The biggest things all of my vocations have had in common, I think, are these two: they all challenged me to sacrifice ego in the service of love; and they all formed my identity, rather than requiring me to form it myself before I was good enough to start the work of love.

That's one reason I have suggested that if you're trying to figure out what to do with your life or what your vocation is, you might look around and see which obligations you *already* have or which ones you long to take on. How would your life look different if you treated your friendships as love relationships? How would your life look different if you thought of yourself as having obligations to your friends? What about obligations to and love for specific people in your community who are in need?

I don't mean that you should be clingy or use others as tools for exploring your own identity or vocation. But if you're trying to figure out how God is calling you to pour out your life in love, maybe one place to start is by *loving*. See whether the relationships that already surround you offer opportunities to love and serve.

The skills you learn through loving and serving—skills of forgiveness, acceptance, service, patience—will serve you well in any and all of your future vocations. They will help you remain grateful and humble during the good times and keep you tender and faithful during the inevitable times of trial or aching loneliness.

There may be a somewhat-transferable skill set, the skills of love: things like recognizing and acknowledging when you've done wrong or listening and being present when you're exhausted, hungry, and feeling wrung out. You'll still need to learn a whole lot of things specific to the individual people you end up serving over the long term, in marriage, your extended family, friendship, religious community, or charity. Those are the changes your vocation will provoke. But there are some ways to prepare yourself for whatever kind of love ends up shaping your life the most. And the best way to learn to love, I think, is learning on the job.

Every Vocation Can Be Lived Badly

For every vocation I describe in this book, there will be a way of turning all its blessings into sins. Take the example of friendship. Friendship can be riddled with jealousy and middle-school-style hierarchies; it can even become *folie à deux*. (Ever seen *Heavenly*

Creatures?) For people with same-sex attraction, same-sex friendships can obviously also present temptations to lust and thereby
to leaving the Church. Our friendships can also be misunderstood
by others, making them think that we're not faithful to Church
teaching when we are. I had the bizarre experience once of being
asked about a woman I'd known for many years.

"Oh, she's my best friend!" I said.

"No, I know, but weren't you guys a couple? I heard that you
were living with your partner."

". . . No, we were never—"

"Not even a little bit?"

Afterward, of course, I told said friend all about it, and we
joked about what on earth "a little bit" might have meant! I said
that I should've told this guy, "Oh sure, I hit it and quit it, but it
was never a big thing, bro."

But many people use this kind of misunderstanding as an
actual argument against gay or same-sex attracted people having
close same-sex friendships, living with friends, or making the
kinds of vows and commitments I'll describe in chapter 7. Was I
"giving scandal" just by having a best friend?[3]

Even asking the question should suggest how much more
pressure there is on vocations of queer people than on vocations
of the heterosexual majority. Very often when I describe possible
ways of living out one's vocations as a gay or same-sex attracted
person, someone will ask me questions that are clearly coming
from a stance in which any form of love expressed by a gay
person is considered to be sexualized by default, and therefore
should be suspect. Excruciating attention is paid to all the ways
these vocations can go wrong without offering any understanding of how fruitful they can be when they go right.

I think it's necessary to be honest about the dangers of all our
vocations, the ways they can be misused and can be twisted into

rationalizations for sin. (That is true of marriage as well. You can use your marriage as a cover for abuse, you can marry someone who shares and strengthens your habitual sins, you can have an "open marriage" or a "child-free by choice" marriage, or your marriage can become obsessive and *folie à deux*. This list is not exhaustive! Everyone knows this, and no one thinks it means heterosexuals shouldn't marry.) And I know I didn't suss out all of the dangers or the best ways to protect against them. We have a *lot* of work to do here. But if, as I describe various ways people have found to live queer lives within Church teaching, you find yourself seeing *only* the dangers, let me suggest that you may have let your prudence harden into callousness or even cruelty. I do think it's cruel to argue that queer people—and only queer people—should have only those vocations that can be lived without fear or temptation. Moreover, *lack* of vocation, lack of an arena in which one can give and receive love, is itself the breeding ground for many sins of despair, resentment, addiction, lust (you don't need to be with another person in order to lust, and in fact being too much alone provokes it), and selfishness. Leading a life without vocation can even give scandal, if scandal is one of your concerns, as it may appear to provide evidence for the lie that a celibate life must be loveless and miserable.

If you let the *perfect* be the enemy of the *good* you will, obviously, end up with neither.

Your Vocation Will Flourish Most When It Is Founded on the Eucharist and Continually Draws You Back to the God Who Is Love

This is the fifth and most important fact about vocation in general. Jesus is our living water, the fountain of love. If we try to love others as a way to lessen our own loneliness or fill some other personal need, we may be tempted to place our own needs above the needs of those we claim to love. We may start to use our friends. We may start to create idolatrous images in our heads of the Perfect Friend or the Perfect Friendship and judge those around us for failing to conform to these images. When we return again and again to the sacraments, especially to the Eucharist, we remind ourselves that our friends can't slake our thirst—only Christ can. Our friends can't heal our wounds. It's not their job. If it's anybody's job, it's Jesus'. This perspective allows us to acknowledge our own needs, rather than pretending we're self-sufficient—but it also guides us away from instrumentalizing our relationships and vocations, turning them into mere medicine.

Every vocation I describe in this book—and also those such as marriage, parenting, and religious life, which I do not describe—comes with a terrible temptation for the ego and usually more than one.

Friendship can become cliquish and gossipy. Friends can be self-centered, demanding more and more of our time and energy while giving little in return. We can try to force children, spouses, and friends to make up for what seems to be lacking in our lives. We can burnish our egos by serving the poor. (And rarely serving them what they actually want. Compare to the lady described in C. S. Lewis's *Screwtape Letters*: "She's the sort of woman who lives for others—you can tell the others by their hunted expression."[4])

All of these dangers are much easier to avoid if we are doing the basics on the spiritual level, the equivalent of brushing and flossing. It's humbling for me to realize how much needier and more annoying I am when I haven't been to confession recently. Confession, Communion, a regular prayer discipline such as a daily Rosary and morning and evening prayer—all of these return us to Jesus and replenish our strength. Prayer and the sacraments give us intimacy with God and keep our love from becoming an ingrown toenail of the soul.

*   *   *   *

A reader wrote me a poignant email that included the question, "Will I still be gay in heaven?"

There are a lot of questions folded within this simple sentence. This is a question about identity and cultural categories, about the meaning of healing and redemption, and about the traces this life will leave on us when we pass to the next. But it's also a question about the nature of human love. How will all our vocations—all our human loves—look when we see God face to face?

In my reply, I noted that one of the few things we know about heaven is that there is no marriage there. In heaven, married love is transformed into some other thing of which it was the shadow or prefiguration.

So too I believe our gay loves and desires may be transformed. Are there any heterosexuals in heaven? I'm not sure the question makes sense. *All* of our human, temporal loves will be transformed there, whether those loves were expressed in this life as marriage, as friendship, or (if there was real love there) as an illicit sexual relationship. Take for example a cohabiting straight couple. In this life, their love is real, deep, and sacrificial, although it also isn't entirely rightly ordered or expressed. In heaven, their love *won't* be transformed into marriage. It will be transformed into something of which marriage was merely the outline. Similarly, I don't think it's very likely that a gay couple's love will become, in heaven, a friendship, even though devoted spiritual friendship might have been the best way for them to express their love in this life. And I definitely don't think that their love will somehow become a heterosexual marriage! I think it's more likely that their love will become something far greater than either marriage or friendship. It will be more beautiful than anything we've seen.

chapter seven
Friendship in
Theology and History

There are few treasures of the Church more beautiful and more forgotten than its theory and practice of friendship. It seems every generation of queer Catholics must rediscover this neglected legacy and be startled by it: the "wedded brothers" buried together in English cemeteries, the vows of kinship taken by friends in the Eastern Church, the intimacy and wry, practical wisdom of St. Aelred's dialogues. In this chapter, I'll look at how same-sex friendship worked in Christian lives of the past. I'll show how it was considered a form of love as deep and spiritually fruitful as marital love and as capable of creating lifelong kinship bonds. Then we'll turn from the past to considerations of the present and future of friendship in the Church: What new challenges does friendship present to us today?

The late historian Alan Bray did more than most to help contemporary Christians see the unexpected beauty in their history and traditions. His 2003 book *The Friend* begins with his investigation of grave markers and monuments, looking for indications of the nature of the relationships between men who were buried together. He found much more than he bargained for. Knights were buried under depictions of their helmets facing each other, as if kissing, with their coats of arms arranged in the same way a sculptor would use to depict the arms of a married couple. Bray began to find evidence not only in tomb markers but in songs, stories, and historical chronicles of a specific form of friendship in which the two friends were described as "wedded brothers." The friends typically swore vows, such as the vow of "true love and brotherhood" sworn by two French knights in the early fifteenth century, and these vows were often crowned by the friends' hearing Mass and receiving the Eucharist together. [1]

The friends, by taking these vows, became kin. Bray wrote: "If the historian of friendship is ready to put aside the unavailing attempt to impose an order on the diversity of evidence about friendship in traditional society, and rather listens to what that diversity is saying, it tells its own story; and the story is among the oldest that humanity has ever told, sitting around the hearth. It is the story of what it means to have a family."[2] Bray goes on to demonstrate that sworn brotherhood was considered a form of kinship based on friendship, chosen by the friends and sealed with vows. He wrote, "Modern society recognizes only one such 'voluntary' kinship, in marriage. In the past others have subsisted alongside it."[3]

Kinship is a form of love that persists after the death of one of the parties. It is a love with obligations as well as joys. With these criteria we can see clearly how medieval sworn friendship differed from the relationship we now describe as being "just friends" with someone. The specific obligations incurred through vows of friendship varied, but they would often include features like caring for the friend's children after death (perhaps an especially important clause given that many of the sworn friends we know of were married knights) and having Masses said for the friend's soul. As Bray put it, "they left each other their families."[4]

Bray also found another form of same-sex kinship formed through promise making. Becoming godparent to a friend's child was one way friends could merge their families' interests and publicly signify their allegiance. As with sworn friendship, kinship created by Baptism drew freely from both blood and marriage kinship for its metaphors and explanations.

The Friend is a beautiful, challenging book, written with great sensitivity and willingness to accept the past on its own terms. Bray was deeply moved by the evidence he found of love between men—and by the story, which he tells in the book, of how that love and intimacy gradually became more and more suspect. There were always dangers in the friendships he describes: the danger that friendship and its obligations would threaten the obligations to wife and children, an anxiety that would get played out in several bloody-minded ballads; or the danger that this friendship, which was presumed to be nonsexual, would become unchaste.

That second danger was present from the beginning. Edward II swore brotherhood with his favorite Piers Gaveston[5], and if you've read your gruesome English history, you know how that story ends. Bray details several cases in which accusations of sodomy were leveled against two men who were friends. In these cases the acts of friendship—sharing a bed, sharing one's secrets—that would ordinarily look normal and honorable could become suspicious only once the men involved crossed class boundaries or were suspected of heresy or treason.

But fear that friendship served as mere cover for sexual sin began to grow in importance through the early modern era. It also continued to be associated with heresy: by the time John Henry Newman became a Catholic cardinal, his deep and abiding friendship with Ambrose St. John had become an object of suspicion and a justification for the fear of effeminacy and homosexuality associated, in the Victorian English mind, with the Catholic Church. Bray's book closes during the age of Newman, one of the last Englishmen who could get away with being buried with his friend like the "wedded brothers" of old.

The use of the term "wedded brother" should suggest the way these vowed friendships borrowed from other kinship forms to express love but aren't reducible to those forms. Even if you believe that two men can be married, it requires a further leap to suggest that brothers can marry each other! This language in itself should suggest what Bray makes clear in his conclusion: that he does not consider these friendships to be gay marriages *avant la lettre*. Describing the less cautious and more controversial work of John Boswell's *Same-Sex Unions in Premodern Europe*, Bray wrote, "As tempers cooled, two major objections to the way Boswell handled his evidence stood out clearly, both of which are right. One is that the expected ideals of the rite would not have comprehended sexual intercourse. The other is that his thesis disguises the fact that the rite did not preclude the individuals involved also being married."[6] Bray viewed Boswell as a pioneer and an influence but took pains to separate his own claims from Boswell's sketchier or more strenuous advocacies.

The need to be clear about what these friendships were not, however, shouldn't blind us to the beauty of what they were. They were as complex as any other human institution and also as prone to misuse. They were sometimes unchaste. They were sometimes purely economic and martial or political arrangements. But they were also something else—found in a fourteenth century chronicle composed by the monks of Westminster Abbey:

> It was also on 17 October that in a village near Constantinople in Greece the life of Sir John Clanvowe, a distinguished knight, came to its close, causing to his companion on the march, Sir William Neville, for whom his love was no less than for himself, such inconsolable sorrow that he never took food again and two days afterward breathed his last, greatly mourned, in the same village.[7]

In the seventeenth century, a monument to the late Dr. Thomas Legge and his friend Dr. John Gostlin was placed in the chapel of Gonville and Caius College at Cambridge University.

The monument, designed by Gostlin, shows Legge kneeling in prayer. Beneath him, "a heart in flames is depicted held aloft by two hands, with the inscription below."[8] The inscription, in Latin, reads, "Love joined them living. So may the earth join them in their burial. O Legge, Gostlin's heart you have still with you."[9] Bray's book delves fully into the ethical dilemmas and practical concerns of friendship—but he never forgets its ardent heart.

Nor does he forget friendship's embodiment. There's a *physicality* to friendship in Bray's book, which comes out most clearly when he discusses the reason that a church setting so frequently recurs in descriptions of friendship.[10] Vows on the church porch, bodies buried together in the chapel—Bray sees here a harmony of the Body of Christ in the Eucharist, the bodies of the saints whose relics are placed under the altar of the church, and the bodies of the friends.

Vows of same-sex friendship existed in both Eastern and Western Christianity. After Boswell's book was published, in which he claimed that these vows represented a kind of "gay marriage ceremony" within the Church, a historian stepped forward to say that she had actually participated in such a vow. Robin Darling Young, writing in the November 1994 issue of *First Things*, like other scholars criticized many of Boswell's translations and interpretations. But she also gave a fascinating description of her own experience of vowed friendship:

> This is a subject about which I have the good fortune to speak not merely as a scholar or an observer, but as a participant. Nine years ago, I was joined in devout sisterhood to another woman, apparently in just such a ceremony as Boswell claims to elucidate in his book. The ceremony took place during a journey to some of the Syrian Christian communities of Turkey and the Middle East, and the other member of this same-sex union was my colleague Professor Susan Ashbrook Harvey of Brown University. During the course of our travels, we paid a

visit to St. Mark's Monastery in Jerusalem, the residence of the Syrian Orthodox archbishop. There our host, Archbishop Dionysius Behnam Jajaweh, remarked that since we had survived the rigors of Syria and Eastern Turkey in amicable good humor, we two women must be good friends indeed. Would we like to be joined as sisters the next morning after the bishop's Sunday liturgy in the Church of the Holy Sepulchre? Intrigued, we agreed, and on a Sunday in late June of 1985, we followed the bishop and a monk through the Old City to a side chapel in the Holy Sepulchre where, according to the Syrian Orthodox, lies the actual tomb of Jesus. After the liturgy, the bishop had us join our right hands together and he wrapped them in a portion of his garment. He pronounced a series of prayers over us, told us that we were united as sisters, and admonished us not to quarrel. Ours was a sisterhood stronger than blood, confirmed in the outpouring of the Holy Spirit, he said, and since it was a spiritual union, it would last beyond the grave.[11]

Discovery of "gay marriage" in the Middle Ages would be pretty shocking. But it is at least equally countercultural to recognize these vows and rituals for what they are: a form of friendship as deep and lasting as any other love.

* * * *

In the premodern worlds of medieval Europe, we can find practices that made friendship a central part of a man's life and vocation. Theology responded to culture by developing and deepening the Christian understanding of friendship's power and purpose.

St. Aelred of Rievaulx was born in the north of England in about the year 1110 to a clerical family. He was fostered by King David I of the Scots and found great success at the Scottish court. But his restless imagination was captured by the monastic life rather than the worldly one, and as a young man, he visited the

recently founded monastery at Rievaulx in Yorkshire. The very
next morning after his visit, he turned up at the gates asking to
become a monk.

Aelred gained support and popularity in his new life just as
he had in the old. He traveled to Rome, meeting and impress-
ing Bernard of Clairvaux (a.k.a. St. Bernard) on his way back,
became abbot at Rievaulx, and traveled widely in support of
the monastic movement. It was during his time as abbot that
he wrote the dialogues that would become *Spiritual Friendship*.
Douglass Roby describes his final hours: "Aelred died, as he had
lived, surrounded by a crowd of his monks."[12]

St. Aelred was renowned for his gentleness and for his care
for all the monks entrusted to him. When a fellow English abbot
heard of his death, he interrupted his sermon to offer this tribute:
"What a honeycomb, how mighty and how rich a one, has passed
in these days to the heavenly banquet. . . . It seems to me that in
him, in his being taken from us, our garden has been stripped,
and has given up a great sheaf of myrrh to God the husbandman.
There is no such honeycomb left in our homes. His discourse was
like the honeycomb, pouring out the honey of knowledge. His
body was languishing with illness, but he himself languished
more from love of heavenly things."[13]

Roby adds his own commentary: "He was a man whose love
was great enough to prove that greatness does not need to be
brutal, and that to be a saint one does not have to despise human
affections."[14]

Although *Spiritual Friendship* does tackle the concerns of
ancient writers on friendship, such as prudence in choosing one's
friends, what stands out to a contemporary reader is the depth
of sacrifice and intimacy St. Aelred recommends for Christian
friendship.

St. Aelred uses Jonathan and David as models for friendship. Jonathan famously loved David "surpassing the love of women"(2 Sam 1:26) and risked his position, his relationship with his father, Saul, and his physical safety in order to stand beside David and support his friend's claim to the kingship. Jonathan made these difficult choices without any hint of hesitation, as far as the biblical narrative tells us. His love for God was channeled through his love for his friend, and in sacrificing material and social well-being for David's sake, he fulfilled God's purposes.

St. Aelred, emphasizing this element of sacrifice, describes Jonathan's love in an extended passage that quotes as its refrain Jonathan's unstinting vow: "You shall be king, and I will be next after you." St. Aelred said—and this excerpt doesn't do justice to the beauty of the passage:

> Never, therefore, prefer yourself to your friend; but if you chance to find yourself the superior in these things which we have mentioned [i.e., worldly goods like rank and riches], then do not hesitate to abase yourself before your friend, to give him your confidence, to praise him if he is shy, and to confer honor upon him in inverse proportion to that warranted by his lowliness and poverty. Jonathan, that excellent youth, paying no heed to a royal crown or to the hope of regal power, entered upon a covenant with David. He made the servant, David, an equal in friendship with the Lord. He preferred him to himself, when David was driven into flight before Saul, when he was hiding in the desert, when he was condemned to death, when he was destined for slaughter; thus Jonathan humiliated himself and exalted his friend. "You," he said, "shall be king, and I will be next after you." O mirror most excellent of true friendship! Marvel of marvels![15]

St. Aelred goes on to call Jonathan "that most loving youth, preserving the laws of friendship, brave in the face of threats, patient before reproaches, despising a kingdom because of his friendship, unmindful of glory, but mindful of grace."[16]

The sacrifices made for friendship become even more prominent when St. Aelred seeks a model in the New Testament. Here we find the most stirring defense of friendship in Christian history in the words of Jesus himself: "Greater love has no man than this: to give his life for his friends" (Jn 15:13). St. Aelred takes these words seriously and adds, "See how far love between friends should extend; namely, that they be willing to die for one another."[17] This comparison can be read as a parallel to the Pauline counsel that husbands should love their wives "as Christ loved His Church," with all the forgiveness and self-sacrifice that line implies (Eph 5:25).

Friendship is sometimes contrasted with sexual love by comparing the images of a romantic couple gazing into each other's eyes and a pair of friends facing outward toward a common goal or project. This imagery distorts both friendship and sexual love, especially marital love. Married couples must often face outward toward their common goal or project (we call some of these projects "children"), rather than remaining enraptured with each other's gaze.

And in St. Aelred, we see that although the friendship of Christians should point beyond itself, to Jesus Christ, friendship can nonetheless be as personal and as deeply interested in the friend for his own sake as any romantic love. Both Book One and Book Two of *Spiritual Friendship* begin with Aelred noting that he was observing his friend quietly while they were in a crowd of others, and he noticed some uneasiness or anxiety in his friend. His close observation and intimate knowledge suggest that the friend himself, not some common project or goal, is the most immediate object of Aelred's attention. The friends are icons to each other, windows through which they can both view Christ;

and their love for each other draws them up into love of Christ.[18] But Aelred does not see this project of mutual improvement in Christian life as detracting in any way from personal, emotional intimacy. Here's how Aelred describes the acts of love which are proper to friendship: "But what happiness, what security, what joy to have someone to whom you dare speak on terms of equality as to another self; one to whom you need have no fear to confess your failings; one to whom you can unblushingly make known what progress you have made in the spiritual life; one to whom you can entrust all the secrets of your heart and before whom you can place all your plans!"[19]

Aelred counsels vulnerability and honesty with one's friends, which is why it's so important to him that friends be selected carefully and even tested beforehand. Aelred wrote, "And yet, not all whom we love should be received into friendship, for not all are found worthy of it. For since your friend is the companion of your soul, to whose spirit you join and attach yours, and so associate yourself that you wish to become one instead of two, since he is one to whom you entrust yourself as to another self, from whom you hide nothing, from whom you fear nothing, you should, in the first place, choose one who is surely fitted for all this."[20] A friend may—in fact, must—unburden his heart by speaking openly and intimately with his friend. Such personal conversations are not distractions from the real project and goals of the friends but rather an important feature of their friendship.

The combination of learned commentary on ancient writers and demanding Christian theology of friendship might make Aelred's dialogues sound too high-octane, an unrealistic picture of life written by a cloistered monk who knew little of the world outside the monastery walls. But *Spiritual Friendship* clearly portrays the day-to-day challenges of friendship. The monks in these dialogues have distinctive personalities. In the first dialogue, Ivo,

Aelred's interlocutor, is an especially beloved favorite; his death occurs in the caesura between the first and second dialogues and affects Aelred deeply. In the second and third dialogues, Aelred is speaking with two different monks: one of them is slightly cynical, another is an eager puppy. They get jealous of Aelred's time ("Gratian has had enough attention already," Walter grouses),[21] and Aelred has to juggle competing responsibilities in order to be with them.

Aelred knows the boring, normal challenges of friendship: there's a good section where he discusses how he handled a friendship in which the friend had a fierce, barely disciplined temper. He also experienced and was formed by its deepest, most personal sorrows. St. Aelred may be writing in a school and style of philosophy that has mostly fallen into disuse, but the kind of friendships he describes should be completely recognizable to a contemporary reader.

Even so, it's not obvious how we could translate his sacrificial and intimate friendship, practiced virtuously and modeled on Christ's love for his disciples, into our own lives. And while Robin Darling Young may have been able to bring medieval friendship vows into the modern world, even Young was not able to replicate the social context in which her vows could be recognized, honored, and understood by those around her.

Has the world in which friendship was a form of love, a type of kinship, and a Christian vocation simply been lost? When I write about knights swearing vows, am I just a gay(er) "Miniver Cheevy, born too late"? In the next chapter, I'll try to prove that we can still learn from these older models of friendship. We can renew them in our own day, although they will present new challenges. A return to traditional Christian understandings of friendship won't "solve the problems" of same-sex love in the postmodern world. But I think it could *change* our problems from less-Christian problems to more-Christian ones.

I don't want to speculate on why Alan Bray included the text of a "Catholic rite for making brothers" in his book. Nor do I think this rite can be simply transplanted from its original Eastern Christian context into contemporary American life. But I will note that it begins on page 130. As the punk slogan said, "If you don't like the news, make some yourself."

chapter eight
Spiritual Friendship Today and Tomorrow

Two are better than one, because they have a good reward for their toil. For if they fall, one will lift up his fellow; but woe to him who is alone when he falls and has not another to lift him up. Again, if two lie together, they are warm; but how can one be warm alone? And though a man might prevail against one who is alone, two will withstand him. A threefold cord is not quickly broken.

—Ecclesiastes 4:9–12

The rewards of friendship could not be more practical. Many studies have (unsurprisingly?) found that friendship is associated with better health outcomes—just like family ties and other forms of social support.[1] I've personally experienced these effects in big and small ways. One summer when I was very sick and feverish, too ill to understand what was going on around me or take care of myself, Meredith took me to the emergency room and stayed with me to make sure I got proper care. Later she also became one of the first people I talked to about my drinking problem, and her support and gentle advice proved to be hugely helpful in addressing what was both a spiritual crisis and, of course, a serious health risk. It is neither possible nor desirable to completely separate most of our vocations from our practical economic and physical needs. Friendship typically offers greater material well-being to the friends even as it satisfies a longing of the heart and soul.

And yet when it comes to gay people, some Christian leaders believe that intimate same-sex friendship is inherently suspect. This overcaution allows fear of the occasions of sin to destroy possible occasions of virtue.

In 2009, Alan Chambers asked if vowed, devoted same-sex friendship was "The New Homosexuality":

> During lunch, my friend asked my views on "covenant friend-ships." I'd never heard that term, but quickly realized she was referring to sexless committed relationships between members of the same gender. I immediately called them sinful. She was shocked. So was I. Apparently, we don't share what I consider to be a fairly cut and dry biblical position on this issue. So I asked her to give me a first-hand account of such a relation-ship that she saw as healthy. She went on to share the story of a Christian lesbian who believes that homosexual behavior is sinful, but holds no hope of ever experiencing heterosexuality. The thought of living a single life was too much for her to bear and so she developed a committed nonsexual relationship with another woman. They held a commitment ceremony, bought a house together, combined their finances and are trying to live happily ever after. They live in separate bedrooms, but in every other sense of the word, they are partners. "What's wrong with that?" my friend asked. Everything.
>
> Talk about selling God short in the "I will supply all of your needs" category. What about abstaining from all appearances of evil? How about fleeing from temptation? Two same-sex attracted women getting married and pledging their lifelong love and devotion to one another, with or without sex, is called homosexuality. How can we say anything less? There is no such thing as diet homosexuality.[2]

Note that the two women in question don't appear to call their own relationship "marriage"—that's an addition by Chambers. For all we know, their "commitment ceremony" was like the one

Robin Darling Young had. They don't sleep together and seem to view their relationship as one of friendship and caretaking, not sex or marriage. It isn't even clear if they're attracted *to each other*, and for that matter, only one of the women is specifically described as experiencing same-sex attraction. And yet because at least one of the two women is same-sex attracted, Chambers viewed the relationship as a form of "diet homosexuality."

Because fear of sexual temptation is the major fear Christians seem to have about same-sex friendships for gay people, I'll address it head-on before going on to what I consider to be more fruitful and more Christian problems that will arise if friendship becomes more central to our lives.

I don't want to minimize the concern. If you're queer and faithful to traditional Christian teaching on chastity, and you fall for your friend, those feelings can be terribly painful. If the friendship becomes a sexual partnership, you may be drawn away from your true vocation into a false facsimile of a vocation. I've seen people get badly hurt in this way; I've seen them lose friendships and lose faith.

The danger is real. But the preventative measure of avoiding intimate same-sex friendship entirely is even worse than the danger. Here are a few reasons to think that avoidance of intimate same-sex friendship is *not* the best approach for someone in contemporary culture who is same-sex attracted.

The first reason is that we all actually do have to learn to have nonsexualized friendships with those of our own sex, and most queer people learn this growing up. I think many straight people use an analogy that doesn't quite work. They'll argue, "If I were struggling with attraction to women I wouldn't seek out hot women to be my 'friends,' and I certainly wouldn't expect my wife or my priest to approve of those friendships!" And these people think that this describes what queer people seeking intimate same-sex friendship are doing. But same-sex friendship is a deep longing in our nature, and one we learn to satisfy in a nonsexual way as part of ordinary psychosexual development.

Gay people have had the experience—that straight people typically have not—of growing up with a lot of nonsexualized contact with the sex we end up finding attractive. Boys and girls typically don't share locker rooms! Queer girls do share them with straight girls. We typically don't stare at them. We instead learn a certain guardianship of the eyes (sometimes from fear of homophobic reprisal, sometimes because we don't want to make them uncomfortable, sometimes because we're shy and uncomfortable ourselves, and sometimes because we just find locker rooms desperately unsexy), and we become used to the experience of *choosing* to leash and manage sexual desire in order to maintain casual relationships and deep friendships that would be disrupted by desire. We're also well aware, of course, that most people are straight, so we're pretty used to the idea of having crushes or attractions that have virtually no chance of being reciprocated. Part of many queer adolescences is the process of learning when you can turn those crushes into lifelong friendships and when you're being needy and projecting your own fantasies onto your crush. So as our sexuality develops, we learn to negotiate a perhaps more complex and nuanced relationship between friendship and eros. Straight people obviously aren't barred from these experiences, and many of them may relate to what I've described here. But queer kids tend to have more of these experiences growing up, since boys and girls are still, rightly, separated in many contexts.

The second reason intimate same-sex friendships are important is that they can help us be more centered in our sexual identities as a woman or a man. I definitely don't believe that all queer people experience insecurity in their gender identity. I've always liked being a girl. (Or a woman, nowadays, since between the ages of thirty and seventy you lose the right to call yourself a "girl.") But for those who do experience this insecurity, close same-sex friendships can be immensely healing. I've had friends tell me that they were profoundly moved and changed by the love they received from (straight, in most cases) same-sex friends, which filled needs for intimacy they hadn't even acknowledged. For at least one friend, filling this need for same-sex *love* sharply reduced the desire for same-sex *sex*. I don't think that happens with everyone—my closest friendships are with women, and yet I am still pretty intensely gay—and "curing homosexuality" is not one of the purposes of friendship anyway. But I do think many gay people have a need for same-sex love, which can be fulfilled even if their sexual desires go unfulfilled; friendship offers the love and beauty without the sin.

And the third reason is a consideration of the alternatives. I feel very confident in stating that *loneliness* provokes more sin among queer people—even more sexual sin—than intimate same-sex friendship. Let's take what might be considered the "extreme" case, in which one or both partners in a sexually active couple becomes Catholic, and the partners attempt to live a chaste life without rejecting each other. Perhaps they even take vows of friendship; they continue to live together.

There are some obvious dangers and temptations here. One commenter at a Catholic website, when I wrote about same-sex friendship vows, compared a same-sex attracted person living with a beloved same-sex friend to an alcoholic living in a bar.

But a bar doesn't love you. A bar doesn't want what's best for you and hasn't pledged to care for you and for your faith, including your chastity. A bar can't salve your loneliness and hunger for love, or encourage you when you're tempted to despair.

I'm one of the people we're supposed to worry about. Some of my closest friendships began based in part on physical attraction. Some of the friendships that helped bring me into the Catholic Church started as crushes.

Most of these women turned out to be straight, which certainly minimized temptation, but to me the more important thing to notice is the way that they offered me forms of support I needed *for my faith*. I've managed to be honest and accountable to these friends in ways I desperately needed. I have sinned much, much more through cutting myself off from their love and help than I ever have through sexual attraction to them.

Over time, the element of sexual attraction has generally become a more aestheticized appreciation; I didn't cultivate the more sexual and especially the more lustful aspects of it, and so it transformed into something much chaster. But even if I were still just as sharply provoked by the sight of my friends as I once was, I'd still argue that the intimate friendship they offered me was much more protective against sin than provocative toward it. There are many sins other than lust in the world: dishonesty, lack of charity, sloth or acedia, self-harm, self-pity, self-centeredness. Loneliness and anxiety—the two things deep friendships most serve to reduce—provoke all of these sins. If I absolutely had to pick one temptation to have, I'd pick temptations to lust over temptations to lies and despair. As it happens, I do think it's often possible to cultivate sublimation of sexual desire and thereby end up without lies, despair, *or* lust, but even within the harshest framing of the question, I don't think the answer is "Avoid friendship with those you find attractive."

* * * *

If we took friendship more seriously, sexual attraction between friends isn't the only problem we'd confront. Some of the other old problems would return. The conflict between loyalty to friend and loyalty to spouse and children was a theme of the old ballads, often expressed with the most gruesomely violent imagery. *The Friend* notes that in one old tale, one friend kills his own children in order to use their blood to magically cure his friend's leprosy; while his wife is at church he "severs the heads of his children, collects the blood, and in that blood as if in a second baptism his friend is saved. God confirms the rightness of his fidelity, the children are restored to life by divine intervention, and—on the day that Amicus is healed—his wife is slain by the devils that have entered her."[3]

Compared to that conflict between friend and spouse, our own "time crunch" or stress looks pretty trivial.

But even without such violence, we might note that time and effort are finite, and spending these resources on a friend's needs may mean spending less of them on one's family. I'm not convinced that things always work this way, with friends and family competing for a limited resource pool. In a fruitful and loving friendship, the friends' support for each other actually strengthens them and gives each of them *more* ability to help those around them, including their families. When we feel supported by our friends, that support can increase our overall energy levels and our desire to serve others. I've seen this dynamic in my own friendships. We make friends a part of our weddings for this reason. A friend at your wedding isn't just having a good time and sharing in your joy; she's also promising to share in your struggles and support your marriage. Thus, the love you share with your friend becomes one of the load-bearing pillars of your marriage.

But there are times when conflict is inevitable. Many single people have noticed that there are stages in which they are mostly giving support to married or marriage-minded friends, rather than receiving it: the stressful run-up to marriage, for example, or the year or so after the first child is born. This imbalance can cause resentment. If you resent your friends for having a family, then that's a problem on your end—one you need to work on in prayer and perhaps spiritual direction. On the other hand, friends can certainly act in self-centered ways that exacerbate resentment. They can seem to take their single friends' support for granted, acting as if our time is less valuable than theirs. They can assume that single friends have no real commitments of our own and are therefore endlessly available for babysitting or hand-holding. And we've all known that one woman who is great *until* she fixates on her new man, at which point she becomes one hundred percent about the boyfriend and zero percent about her women friends.

These conflicts will probably increase as friendship becomes more important in your life, since you will have rejected our culture's answer: the answer that you should obviously sacrifice friendships for romantic relationships. Right now, we pretty much assume that the only relationships worth sacrificing for are romantic or parental ones. It's normal to turn down a better job to be closer to your family, but it would seem weird and clingy to do the same thing to stay close to friends. Taking time off from work to care for ailing spouses, children, and relatives is not only recognized in culture but protected in law; the same actions to care for a friend go silently unnoticed.

These acts of care for friends fill the literature of the AIDS epidemic. They also appear in the literature of combat veterans. Jonathan Shay, in his groundbreaking study *Achilles in Vietnam: Combat Trauma and the Unmaking of Character*, wrote:

> Many individuals who experience friendship as one of the central goods of their lives find that their employers will not recognize philia between people whose relationship is not

familial. Veterans have lost their jobs because they left work to aid another veteran, in circumstances where the same absence would have been "understandable" and charged against sick or vacation time had the other been a spouse, parent, or child. Many people today view friendship purely as a leisure activity, or a sweetener that with luck arises among co-workers, neighbors, or members of a voluntary association such as a church or club but which will be put aside if it gives rise to any conflicting claims at work. Many veterans have also alienated their spouses because they would leave home to go to the aid of fellow veterans. The ancient Greeks, perhaps because their societies were so highly militarized (every male citizen was also a soldier), simply assumed the centrality of philia.[4]

The more we begin to respect and honor sacrificing for one's friends, the more of that sacrifice we'll get—and the more, therefore, those sacrifices will be seen to compete with the care demanded by family and other commitments.

Empathy is the boring, obvious, and essential practice that can make friendship and marriage support each other rather than compete with each other. Singles, especially those whose commitments don't involve demanding physical and emotional labor within our own homes, need to remember that married and parenting friends can feel like their tasks and burdens are endless and inescapable. We may have more of a refuge to retreat to when things get difficult, and so we have a responsibility to provide peace and refuge for our friends.

For single laypeople who live alone, it might be worth asking: Are there ways I could get a little closer to offering the on-call love my married and parenting friends so often must provide? Are there times when I hold myself back from others because I'm too attached to my own freedom, the pleasure of my own company, and the security of my own plans and preferences? Do I choose ways of helping and giving that are more gratifying to my ego, such as giving advice or selecting presents I know they'll enjoy and praise, but avoid the boring or gross tasks of love like making casseroles and learning to burp infants? Could I live the more demanding and chaotic life of the person who has a *duty* to love?

And the even tougher question: When I want to give more, or differently, than another person wants to receive, can I let go of my self-image and my own need to be useful? Even our desire to give can become an imposition if we focus too much on our own need to be needed.

On the other side of the fence, where the grass is always being eaten by the kids, empathy would require recognizing when your friend is making a sacrifice in order to be there for you. A friend who is available for emergency childcare is doing something notable, and a little praise and gratitude can go a long way. A friend who gives up her own plans in order to take you out to coffee when you need to cry over relationship trouble may not be making as obvious a sacrifice as you have, but she's also giving of herself freely. During the most absorbing and challenging times of your marriage and parenting, you may not be able to give yourself as fully or obviously to your friend as she's giving herself to you, and that's fine. Love isn't about equality or keeping score. But you can honor her gift of self rather than acting as if you're entitled to it.

If you're an employer, you can also exercise empathy here. Ask yourself: If I wanted to support my employees' love and care for others, not limiting them to caring for their spouses and children, how would I do that? Are there ways I can help them to knit together a broader fabric of support? Communal bonds like friendship require care and present us with duties; they also strengthen us and help us cope with life's difficulties. An employer who recognized both the sacrifices and the benefits of friendship might find some way of accommodating employees who want to serve their friends as they would serve relatives in need. I hesitate to make specific recommendations, since employers and employees will know their own needs best. But it's worth asking: How can I support my employees' friendships, where they are truly forms of sacrificial love, rather than forcing those friendships to compete with the demands of the workplace?

*   *   *   *

While friendship can conflict with particular other love relationships, such as marriage, it can also present a weirder and more purely postmodern challenge to the *institution* of marriage. This was not a conflict faced by medieval knights. A 2012 *New York Times* story lays out the possible problem in a feature on four men who live together in a kind of beguinage of bros:

> They have no children, no linear career histories, no readily disposable savings. The four men, all heterosexual, approaching forty and never married, have lived together for eighteen years, give or take a revolving guest roommate, cohabitating in spaces like an East Village walk-up, a Chelsea loft and, now, a converted office space in Queens. . . . Sociologically, the men represent the apotheosis of two trends in American life. While Mayor Michael R. Bloomberg may be promoting the idea of tiny apartments for singles, the most recent census figures suggest that many people do not want to live alone; they prefer or need the company: The number of roommates in nonfamily households in New York City increased by more than forty percent between 2000 and 2010. At the same time, Americans, especially men, have been pushing back the age at which they first marry—for men, it climbed to 28.2 years in 2010, up from 26.8 a decade earlier. One of the men explains his life this way: "We've somehow

drifted into this place where we are really close, and care about each other deeply, and yet we give each other lots of space and stay out of each other's daily business. . . . We've got all the benefits of a family with very little of the craziness that normally comes along with them."[5]

In a divorce-traumatized culture with an intense fear of commitment, friendship may offer a form of love that is temptingly flexible. Because there are so many different levels of friendship, it lends itself to easing into things rather than big dramatic decisions. There's (rightly) much less judgment if you break a friendship than if you break your wedding vows, and there are far fewer concerns about betrayal. Nobody thinks you're "cheating on" your best friend if you begin to get closer to another friend. There are far fewer rules and societal expectations associated with friendship, so it's adaptable to individual needs—and it offers plausible deniability for the unscrupulous ones who are content to receive support from others without offering it themselves. So friendship, precisely because it's genuinely loving and supportive, may present itself as an easier alternative to marriage.

Where marriage has weakened, other forms of kinship can often be strengthened to fill similar roles—to a limited extent and for a little while. As I've worked with poor urban women who come to the pregnancy center, I've been struck by how many of them take being a godmother or a godsister very seriously. You're expected to listen to your godmother, turn to her for advice, and offer her especial respect and honor. You're supposed to give your godsister both emotional and financial support; she truly becomes a sister to you. Relationships between cousins also seem much stronger in these communities than in the upper-class ones I come from. Necessity can forge social bonds in which kin are relied on more because they're needed more.

The sociologist Karen Walker, describing differences between
working-class friendships and upper-class ones, wrote that working-class friendships tend to be more durable. They form lasting networks of obligation. Upper-class friendships are more
based on shared interests and tend to fade away when one friend
moves—since upper-class people are more mobile.

Walker cautions that it's easy to sentimentalize these more
interdependent working-class friendships:

> Given the findings in this study, it is tempting to idealize the
> working-class patterns of exchange and reciprocity in an overly
> individualistic society. But the flip side to the positive interde-
> pendence is conflict and resentment over whether someone
> owes someone else a favor. In addition, the concern over repu-
> tation and privacy among the working-class respondents was
> sometimes overwhelming. It is also tempting to idealize mid-
> dle-class patterns of friendship if one is interested in self-devel-
> opment and the expression of individuality. But middle-class
> friendships sometimes left respondents feeling isolated and
> alone. For the middle class, times of trouble are times when
> friendship, whose focus is shared interests and leisure, may
> not survive.[6]

Sentimentality of working-class relationships also crept into earlier writing about familial and community bonds in poor black
neighborhoods. Picking up a sociology text from the '70s, one
might get the impression that it's perfectly fine if black children
grow up without knowing their fathers, since they have cousins
and godmothers instead. And some theorists who seek to recognize the claims and bonds of friendship actively argue that
they're seeking to relativize marriage, so it becomes just one kind
of relationship among many other equal competitors.[7]

Depending on what the concept means, "relativization" of
marriage may indeed be needed. Many Christian authors have

pointed out that idolizing marriage, especially in the romantic and individualistic way we do today, isn't true to the much more radical Gospels. Jesus wasn't married. He didn't say, "There is no greater love than this: to lay down one's life for one's wife," or even "one's children." He *did* say, "If any man come to me, and hate not his father, and mother, and wife, and children, and brethren, and sisters, yea, and his own life also, he cannot be my disciple" (Lk 14:26). And many of the early saints, such as St. Agnes and St. Lucy, were women martyred for their refusal of marriage in favor of becoming brides of Christ.

But saying "We often make marriage an idol" isn't to say "We don't need marriage," any more than pointing out that we often make churchgoing or "religion" an idol means that Christians shouldn't go to church. There are, obviously, many instances when friendship, godparenthood, and other forms of love, no matter how genuine, sacrificial, and real, can't substitute for marriage. They don't fulfill the unique needs marriage fills (or should fill), such as regulating sexual behavior or keeping men in the home with their children. If the strengthening of alternative forms of kinship such as godparenthood or vowed friendship comes at the expense of marriage, it's not worth it.

I believe these forms of relationships can strengthen one another. We can exalt friendship and godparenthood or god-siblinghood bonds without pretending that marriage thereby becomes less necessary. In fact, we may be able to call upon friendship to strengthen our marriage culture.

In my work at the pregnancy center, I've shifted more and more toward trying to knit women and their children into whatever part of their social fabric seems strongest. The project of fostering love from a mother to her unborn child, and between that child's mother and father, turns out to be part of a much larger project of uniting or reuniting the woman with her own mother, perhaps with her godparents, her grandparents, a church, or her friends. Each of these bonds, once strengthened, can give the woman hope that she can then bring to bear on the places where she lacks support.

It's possible to recognize the importance of marriage and family unity while also looking for all the other places in our lives where we can build a civilization of love.

Many problems—of jealousy, resentment between friends, and competition between the "institution" of friendship and the institution of marriage—may be ameliorated simply by our becoming aware of them. Friends might remind themselves that supporting each other's *other* relationships and ties is a part of their job as friends. Being a good friend includes being the kind of friend who you'd want to hold your *chuppa*, the Jewish wedding canopy, and it also includes being the kind of friend who can help his friends make it to the altar. If we do manage to renew the practice of friendship vows for unusually dedicated pairs—and I hope we do, since I find that practice truly beautiful—the new wave of vows might include explicit promises to support the friend's marriage or other family ties.

Vowed friendships, and in fact any friendships, can't simply be transplanted from medieval England to contemporary America. This question of competition between marriage and friendship suggests one way today's friendships are likely to be starkly different from the friendships Bray and St. Aelred describe: today, friends often inhabit very different vocations and life stages for a long time. We're not talking about a monk whose friends are all also monks. We're talking about a lay person, unmarried and perhaps not seeking marriage, whose friends may be married, looking for a spouse, in religious life, or also single and not looking.

The friends may also have widely varying religious beliefs. This is a challenge St. Aelred had no reason to address—his work assumes that friends share basic religious and cultural assumptions, even if they vary in how well they live out their faith. He takes as a baseline Cicero's ideal that friends should enjoy "mutual harmony in affairs human and divine."[8] This is not a bar that many of my closest friendships come anywhere near reaching. Many of my closest friends, including Meredith, aren't Christian. So these days I try to take a "keep your own side of the street clean" approach: my job isn't to convert my friends. This perspective is the result of painful experience. The times when I've tried to convert them stand out as times when I've been unusually self-centered rather than Christ-centered in my approach to them. My job is to maintain my own relationship with God, through prayer and frequent confession and Communion.

Spiritual friendship across the lines of faith and doubt may turn out to be harder in theory than in practice. Or the divide of religious faith may be too great for many people who would otherwise be able to form bonds of loving friendship. Many of my non-Christian gay friends have become much more distant from me as our beliefs and life paths diverged. This separation has been painful for me, and I've tried to prevent it, but it's obvious why such a friendship might face powerful stresses.

I don't know that I have especially good advice for people seeking to forge strong friendships across religious lines. I'd definitely caution the religious person to be aware of how often religious faith has been used to bully or pressure others and be sensitive to any signs that you're doing that to your friend. I wish I had been much more sensitive to the times when I was calling up painful memories for my friends or simply acting as if I were obviously in the right and they were obviously in the wrong.

Other than that, I can only offer the conviction that it is possible to compromise on neither faith nor love—but what that looks like will be different in each relationship.

In *The Friend*, Alan Bray notes, "There is no more revealing question about the friendship of traditional society than to ask how it encompassed women."[9] He found no evidence that before the seventeenth century women were able to forge the kind of *public*, "formal" and "objective" friendships men had. Although women did eventually enter into the vows and rituals of friendship, there's still a lot of exploration to be done on the question of whether it makes sense simply to incorporate women into vows and rituals initially designed for men's friendships. Women in the West have our own lost traditions of "romantic friendship," and these traditions may offer a few differences from men's friendships—for example, the "Boston marriage."[10] I have no personal opinion on the question of whether and how women's same-sex friendships differ theologically from men's; I find the rituals of both Western and Eastern churches quite beautiful, and don't think the Western models need to exclude women. The Eastern models don't.

Postmodern life poses the question of cross-sex friendship in a way premodern life did not. If vows of chaste friendship became more common (or, more accurately, less entirely unheard-of) some people might ask whether they could vow friendship to an opposite-sex friend in whom they had no romantic interest. Could a husband have both a wife and a female vowed friend? My traditionalist instinct is to say no. Vowed friendship should remain what it has always been in the past, a same-sex institution. Vowed friendship between people who *could* take marriage vows seems to me to carry stronger possibilities of sexualization than if the vows are only for pairs who could not marry in the Church. I also think, as I described above, that most queer people have already learned a lot about negotiating nonsexual relationships with members of the same sex by the time they reach adulthood, whereas straight people, due to the ordinary developmental patterns of childhood, are less likely to have practiced the skill of nonsexual friendship with the opposite sex.

Beyond the perhaps outré and distracting question of explicit vows, however, there's a lot of work to be done on cross-sex friendship in Christian thought and practice. We have many models of deep friendship between men and women saints—St. Francis and St. Clare come to mind. However, many of these friendships were between vowed monastics, which place them in a very different social context from the guy whose best friend is a woman he works with at Taco Bell. I'm not the right person to do this work; I mostly gravitate toward women for friendships and I definitely feel like I understand those friendships better than my friendships with men. So I want to flag this as an area in which ancient and medieval models may be unhelpful or silent, even though I don't have anything useful to say myself.

*   *   *   *

Friendship, perhaps more than any of the other vocations I'll discuss in this book, can go beyond merely coexisting with other vocations. It frequently strengthens them. Art can be greedy, service to others can be exhausting, and community can be overwhelming. Marriage and religious vocations can be deeply isolating and, parenting, famously, is basically an eighteen-year boot camp of sleeplessness and terror shot through with wonder. While I don't want to downplay the drama, loneliness, or jealousy that can sometimes disrupt and weaken friendship, I do find that in my own life it is most often a source of replenishment. Time spent with friends can be the "shade and sweet

water" we need in order to go out into the world and pursue
our other callings.

But where can we find these friendships, and how can we
foster them?

chapter nine

From Friends to Family

Many people who want the spiritual friendships I've described have a hard time figuring out where to find them. So here are some theories, examples, and practical suggestions on the question of finding friends. All of these are things I or other people have tried that have worked for us. As with all advice, there may be terrific reasons you haven't done them already, and my goal is not to make you feel bad because you haven't found the relationships you want. Take what's useful to you here, and leave the rest.

How to Choose a Friend

All of the classical writers on friendship addressed the question of choosing a friend. St. Aelred devotes a good portion of his third dialogue to it. And if friendship becomes more important and more honored in our society, I suspect this question will increase in importance as well.

Today we hear almost nothing about it. We hear a lot about how to pick a marriage partner—maybe we even hear too much. Our marriage culture, such as it is, focuses on the quest for the perfect soul mate. We have skewed too far toward emphasis on making the exact right decisions on the front end rather than emphasis on learning the skills of flexibility, acceptance of change, forgiveness, repentance, and loyalty that will be necessary in the long years *after* the wedding. So we may be overly obsessed with picking the right spouse. But we are perhaps insufficiently obsessed with picking the right friends. Certainly that's what St. Aelred and Aristotle would think if they could see the haphazard, amoral ways we tend to slide in and out of friendships.

For St. Aelred it was important to choose friends wisely *because* they were so central to one's vocation and one's spiritual development. St. Aelred didn't demand perfection before he would give himself in friendship. In fact, he suggested that people who recognize their own character defects and struggle against them could make the best possible friends.[1] He discusses his friendship with a hot-tempered monk, and makes it clear that even when character defects have been revealed in the friend, true friendship demands loyalty and gentleness in addressing those defects.

Nonetheless, St. Aelred dismisses the low-rent, workaday motives of convenience or casual companionship by which many of us actually choose our friends. He challenges us to examine potential friends as we might examine potential spouses, *because* he plans to trust these friends and sacrifice for them, and remain loyal to them for life.

I admit that I don't think I've ever practiced St. Aelred-style testing of potential friends. I more or less wake up inside my friendships, only noticing them once they've already been forged too tightly to easily slither out of them. My friendships tend to be based on shared experiences rather than shared belief, and the experiences themselves are not exactly morally edifying. "We got drunk and argued about philosophy a lot" isn't a basis for friendship that St. Aelred would approve or even necessarily understand, and yet it's served me well so far.

St. Aelred may be too idealistic. The ballads of knights and their friends, and the descriptions of vowed friendship found in Bray's book, spent little time describing moral and spiritual criteria for choosing a friend. When any criteria were mentioned, they tended to involve considerations of advantage (political allegiance or family advantages, such as making sure one's children were cared for) or the physical proximity and shared experience of men in arms. Despite these humble motives for friendship, the friendships themselves could become emotionally deep and spiritually fruitful; as in marriage, lifelong loyalty could be borne from necessity or convenience. Sometimes we love someone for the same reason George Mallory climbed Everest—because she was there.

But I don't want to push my own position too much, because this is a question where I'm still uncertain. Maybe we need a revival of the friend-choosing manual. I'm definitely the wrong person to write it. I understand how to try to change and grow with one's friends and how to cope with disappointment if they choose not to make an effort to keep you as a friend. I have some sense of how to cope with the realization that a friend wants more from you than you were prepared to give—the realization that the other person wanted spiritual friendship when you were only hoping for companionship. Those long-term skills are things I've experienced. The short-term skills of choosing a good friend are things I've basically ignored.

Dan Barden is the author of *The Next Right Thing*, a terrific, funny, and insightful noir novel set within Southern California's addiction-recovery community. In an interview, he said:

> What I know about Alcoholics Anonymous is that it's very much about caring about people you shouldn't care about. A.A. was started when this stockbroker [Bill W.] from New York went to Ohio on a business trip. He was afraid he was going to drink and so he started calling people and saying, "Listen, who's the worst alcoholic here?" And they said, "This guy Dr. Bob's really bad," and Bill said, "Okay, I want to talk to him." His solution was that he could help himself with his own alcoholism by helping a hopeless person. So in some ways, recoveries from alcoholism can be said to be about choosing poorly in your friends.[2]

This is more or less the opposite of St. Aelred's perspective. It's also the perspective I'm most deeply drawn to. But I realize I may be drawn *too* much toward the "acceptance of what's given" model of friendship rather than the "choice" model.

My blundering approach to friendships is highly untraditional and quite possibly unwise. But even I did take some actions that were intended to help me find friends and keep the ones I've found. Here are some of the things that have been helpful for me and might be for you.

First of all, you have to throw a few handfuls of glitter into the void. You have to put yourself out there! If you go to an event hosted by your youth ministry, or the gay and lesbian ministry if there is one (this is how I met some very good friends), and someone says something you like, mention it to them. Maybe ask if they want to grab coffee. I have several friendships that started online; we discussed something I had written or something they had written and then decided to meet face to face. Don't be pushy, but don't be shy. You won't get anywhere by hoping in silence, and you have to risk rejection in order to find friends.

Second, I've been pretty intentional about apologizing and forgiving. It's so easy to lose friends. I've managed to maintain friendships with some fairly prickly people whom I love, even though I'm moody and difficult myself; a big part of why I still have those friendships is that I apologized a lot and I forgave them a lot. Friendships deepen over time, as with all forms of love. If you don't stick it out when it's tough you will never get to the long-term, lasting trust that can come from knowing the other person has seen you at some catastrophically low points and loves you anyway.

And third, I organize and initiate. This may seem like a little thing, but seriously, throw parties. Invite people to things. Suggest coffee or dinner. Don't be resentful if you do most of the party throwing or fun making in your circle of friends. I mean, somebody has to. A very wise man in my college debate society once said, "When you don't know what to do, throw a party."

Friendship with Married Couples

For many single people, forming deeper friendships will mean forming friendships with married couples and/or parents. The friends you met in college begin to form families, or you go out in the world and mostly meet people in a different walk of life from your own. These friendships can pose unique challenges— though they also offer unique joys. The single person can feel like an adjunct, an observer, a burden, a mere set of helping hands, or an asymmetrical outcropping on the harmonious family—a poor relation. But when single people are truly drawn into families we can experience a lot of the joys of family life and help parents and spouses bear their own burdens.

Wesley Hill has some even better suggestions. Riffing on a *New York Times* article about the difficulties of forming deep friendships after age thirty, he wrote:

> When I speak to groups of Christians about celibacy and friendship, one of the questions that always comes up is whether intimate friendships are attainable in churches today, particularly for single young adults. "You speak positively and hopefully about friendship," people say, "but are you and other celibate gay Christians actually satisfied by the friendships you've found? Do you have the companionship and intimacy you need?" This NYT essay points to some reasons for skepticism on that front. And if emotionally fortifying friendships aren't attainable for young adult Christians, then is celibacy really a viable option for those Christians? Outside of religious orders, where proximity, regular unplanned interactions, and a setting that nurtures meaningful speech and mutual self-disclosure seem more readily available, where are

the kinds of friendships that will sustain "parish celibacy" (which is the way I've started referring to the Christian practice of celibacy outside of vowed religious contexts, etc.)? I don't have a good answer to this question, other than to talk about what has been sustaining to me. (And also to admit, candidly, in many ways, in the words of U2, "I still haven't found what I'm lookin' for.") . . . [M]y post-college friendships with married people have each involved frequent *planned* interactions. I think of the middle-aged couple with teenage children at my church in Minnesota with whom I had lunch (that stretched into dinner) every Sunday afternoon. I think of the couple my age who lived next door to me in England. We attended the same church, and we had a standing Wednesday dinner appointment. Throughout the week, there would be other spontaneous times of seeing one another, but we always knew that on Wednesday at least, we'd be together. Likewise with another couple I was close friends with in graduate school: every Tuesday night we'd alternate cooking for each other—I'd be at their house one week, they'd come to mine the next week. Again, I'd see them at other times—often several times a week, and on weekends—but we knew we could count on significant time together at least once a week. Being able to count on these interactions, rather than having to expend the energy each week to schedule time together with friends, gave me a great deal of emotional security. Third, the "after 30" friendships that I've made with married people have all depended in large measure on my married friends' treating me not as a frequent guest but like an uncle to their children. While in Durham, two of my close couple friends asked me to be a godfather to their children. Being a godparent doesn't necessarily (or even often, in our culture, I guess) guarantee frequent interaction, but in my case, it meant that I was with these two couples so much that it began to seem natural for me to go on family outings with them, to read books to their children before bedtime, even to share in household chores. I suspect many single Christians feel out of place in churches that place such a premium on programming for families in part because many families are not prepared to welcome single people as permanent members of their circle. But in my case, in Durham at least, I didn't feel that dichotomy—between couples (or singles) with children and (childless) single people—as sharply as I might have because my close parent friends made clear to me that they considered me part of their family.[3]

Hill goes on to note that just as his married and parenting friends opened their homes to him, he likewise opened his to them: "I might add here that I also, as a single person, didn't consider parents with young children outside of *my* circle. I regularly invited families over to my house for dinner, and there were other single people in my church who did the same."

It makes a big difference if you're welcoming to people *as* families with their kids. I'm not great with children—I'm ideologically in favor of them, but they can be kind of hard to talk to—but fostering friendship with families means overcoming that weakness. It means making kids feel *welcome* in your home, not like intruders. And that means giving up a lot of the perks that come with single life. It means accepting that milk will get spilled on your carpet, and your nice things will get teethed on and puked on. (This happens with some adult friends too, of course.) It means dividing your attention between fascinating conversation and "Mars *is* a planet! What's your favorite planet?" It means being a little unfocused, a little gross, and a lot forgiving. This is the price of admission to friendship with parents. It is totally worth it, but be prepared.

In fact, a big part of fostering deep and sacrificial friendship is willingness to let go of some of the good stuff single people sometimes get to keep. I'm still working on this. I enjoy my own

company, and I can get very protective of my time. But having a
true friend means that when she calls, if you possibly can pick up
the phone you always do. It means her needs trump your plans.

As single people, we don't always control our schedules and
our lives, and married people and parents often underestimate
how tied down we really are. If you're working two jobs, caring
for an aging parent, and/or "on call" with a service to those in
need, you are probably not living the footloose and fancy-free
bachelorette lifestyle your envious married friends may envision.
But if you *do* have a good amount of control of your time and
your surroundings, surrendering that control may be the best
thing you can do for your friendships.

Surrender control in favor of love: It's probably obvious how
this might improve your spiritual life.

The rewards of a friendship that become kinship accrue
for single people—but also for their married friends. And the
rewards of love spill beyond the adult friends themselves, as
a single person befriends and becomes part of an entire family.
Knitting single people more closely into families is one of the
biggest things the Christian churches could do to change the
culture.

What does it look like? I'll quote a lay Christian on a blog
called *Gay Subtlety*. He described the joy and gratitude he felt as
a groomsman at a friend's wedding, and then wrote:

> A quick observation about the bride and groom: they have
> served as an example of how single people (specifically those
> who are gay) can be woven into the fabric of a married couple's
> life together. After I came out to the groom, he sent me a letter
> explaining how, even should I never have a family of my own,
> I had to know that I would always be a part of theirs—that I
> was someone they wanted their kids to know and learn from.
> They have demonstrated that their love for each other some-
> how includes me. I can't quite explain it, but I know it to be

true, and as I rejoiced over them with friends new, old, and unintroduced, I caught the slightest glimpse of a future spent never too far from a warm living room full of people who will gladly call me brother and friend.[4]

chapter ten

The Church as Home

We give up the temptation to move from place to place in search of an ideal situation. Ultimately there is no escape from oneself, and the idea that things would be better someplace else is usually an illusion. And when interpersonal conflicts arise, we have a great incentive to work things out and restore peace. This means learning the practices of love: acknowledging one's own offensive behavior, giving up one's preferences, forgiving.

> —from the vows of the Mississippi Abbey,
> a Benedictine community

Americans typically have a difficult time thinking in terms of community. We're much more comfortable picturing atomized individuals, with maybe an overarching state to make us all play nicely with one another. Even when we expand this vision to imagine humans loving one another, we tend to picture two people forming a unit on their own. The basic family unit is, depending on your class background, either two adults forming a romantic couple or a woman and her child.

When I was a young punk, I met a few people living in what were called "collectives." (One of them was even called the Beehive Collective, which seems slightly irony impaired, but maybe they did that on purpose.) Life in the collective seemed to be one-half party planning and one-half emotional drama about who left the fridge open. I have come to believe that this is actually a fairly accurate and hopeful representation of community life. It's not a bad ratio, spending half of your time on the actual purpose of your community—I say "party planning," but the music shows were typically benefits for social causes, as well as opportunities for people to forge friendships in the broader punk community and to sell their records and punk magazines, in addition to having a good time. And drama management is inherent in any group living situation—from the monastery to the family.

The punk collectives offered (usually temporary) love and meaningful work. They offered the kind of friendship that is more like family: the kind that can last through stupid fights and serious fights and the kind in which you sometimes feel like you're stuck with each other. This was a *benefit* of the collectives, not a drawback. Even actual, avowed anarchists can't sustain community life without sacrifice, rules, and constraint.

And so the punk collectives could look a little bit like convents without Christ. What does it look like when you keep the countercultural edge but devote the community to serving God? It might look something like the Christian "intentional community" movement.

These are communities in which lay people live together, typically make decisions together, and attempt to serve God in ways they believe contemporary mainstream culture overlooks. They often live in urban or rural poor areas, making neighbors of those in need. They often draw inspiration from the book of Acts and the lives of the early Christians; one subset of the movement calls itself "the new monasticism," seeking inspiration from a later part of the Christian past. They have names like Bethlehem Farm, Bread and Roses, Center for the Working Poor/Burning Bush Community, and A Simple House.

"Intentional community" covers a broad spectrum, and it's hard to generalize even about intentional Christian communities. I've met people in Catholic communities and people in Protestant

ones; people who plan to spend a couple of years in the community, people who plan to live in the community until they marry,
and people who have pledged to remain with their community
for life. Some communities require that those who live there pro-
fess Christian faith, while others are spurred and guided by faith
but don't require that all members share it.

I am not the best person to present community life as a vocation. In my initial outline for this book, I summarized this chapter
as, "This is fun for other people, I guess." But I wanted to begin
the chapter on community in general with life in an intentional
community because this is a place where people live out alternatives to individualist American Christianity. Specifically, the
intentional communities provide alternatives to the nuclear or
post-nuclear family that our culture presents as the only intelligible vocation—the only way to become (finally) an adult. For
some people these communities will simply provide experiments
in living, places where they can learn to love and sacrifice before
they go on to more ordinary adult vocations. But for others community life may be a lifelong calling.

Tim Otto, a gay man living in a community in San Francisco,
has found in Christian community a vocation and a home. I inter-
viewed him about life in community—the joys, the humiliations,
and the path to discernment. As with any vocation, no flowery
description can substitute for a real-life model; here's one.

**ET: What is your living situation right now *like*—phys-
ically, what do you do all day?**

TO: The community I'm part of is called Church of the
Sojourners. We have about thirty-five people and that
includes eight kids. We have a pretty good age range. I
think our oldest member is seventy, and we have someone who's pregnant right now. The youngest kid is three.

We try and live in households. So generally, we'll have a family living with one or two single people. I live in a house with three other single people. One of them is an older lady, and she struggles with the noise and chaos of kids, so we created a house without kids.

In terms of the rhythm of the week, we have morning prayers every morning. It's just fifteen minutes long, but we gather every morning and pray together. We eat dinner as a household three nights a week, and on Sunday mornings we have what we call "sabbath time," which is when we try to basically be quiet and find a way of being in communion with God. We have a worship time each week. We have a Bible study teaching time each week.

Three weeks out of each month we have what we call a "discernment meeting"; that's where we discuss how we live together. We used to call it a "business meeting," but we realized that the purpose of it was to try to seek God's will rather than our own. But that's the time when we consider everything from the need for a new car to our resources for hosting guests. We discuss all the things that come up in community. We do have a leadership group, but what the leadership does is try to take care of the small things and then figure out what are the bigger things that we need to discuss as a group.

And so most of us work normal jobs. I work as a nurse. There are people who work as teachers, social workers, and people who work in information technology. It's a way of being family to one another and trying to make that image that's so common in the New Testament real.

ET: How did you discern to do that?

TO: A lot of it was thinking about my sexuality. I spent a year in Central America, and a lot of that time I was alone or with people I knew very briefly. And I think at the heart of our sexuality is a desire to not only *be* loved. We realize that loving *other* people is what we were made for.

I already knew some of the people involved with this particular community, and some of them were older Christians who were mentors and who had loved me really well, so I moved to San Francisco not sure what I wanted to do with my life; and at one of the first meetings here I said, "I'm gay and I'm a Christian, and I really don't know how those things go together." We spent the next few years reading books together and talking and ultimately made a decision that if I was going to stay here, I would need to be celibate.

But what happened in that process was that I realized that people had structured their lives in a way that they had time for me; and they loved me really well. I felt loved, and I felt challenged to love [in ministries like the community's provision of emergency housing].

An opportunity to love is a little bit of a crucible. It's creating a situation where you have to learn the arts of love, in some sense.

For one thing, when I was in college I started reading some liberation theology, and became more aware of God's concerns for the poor and oppressed. So I had this image of myself as somebody who cared about the poor and oppressed. And it's one thing to go and help in a soup kitchen for a couple hours a week in order to feel good about yourself, but it's quite another thing to live down the hall from someone! And I realized that loving the poor is not very sexy. It's very mundane. One way it helped me grow is it helped me see through some of my own self-conception and some of the illusions I had about myself.

The other thing that I would say about community is—somebody told me this as a quote—something like, "Whatever you are seeking in community, you will not find in community. All you will find is more reason to give yourself to God."

And that's true. Knowing that I wasn't going to get married, I was kind of looking for guaranteed friends. And some of that has been true of community, but it's actually been much harder than I would ever have guessed to have significant friendships in this context. I think community brings you close enough together that you inevitably see the brokenness in each other. Not only do you see it, but because you're living together, it inevitably affects you. In some friendships you can kind of titrate the relationship in some ways and shield yourself from parts of the other person that maybe are damaging or unhealthy; but it's harder to do that in community. I think community attracts people like myself who are broken and for some reason don't fit in. So in some sense it's a group of misfits trying to love each other, and that brings with it its own challenges.

ET: How were you raised?

TO: My parents were missionaries and my dad was a pastor. They were Baptists. A very religious home, a very good home in many ways. So there was a sense growing up that you need to take Christianity really seriously; and yet being gay, I didn't think I could do the typical things like be a missionary or a pastor. It seemed to me that [community life] is a way of trying to give my life completely to God.

My parents were actually remarkably supportive of me. My mom said eventually, after she understood more about it, "You know, the thing that helped me out of my own selfishness was the constant demands of kids and being married. So I'm glad you've found a context which draws you out of your selfishness." Which is kind of a harsh thing for a mother to say, but it's true!

ET: You mentioned that you discerned how to live out your sexuality *with* your community. What was that like?

TO: Well, it was about twenty years ago! Maybe kind of like you describing [your own] process of becoming Catholic, there were so many factors going on, and not all of them things I'm completely proud of. I think mostly I experienced it, actually, as an act of love—just in that I grew up in a small town in the early '80s, and homosexuality was so—my best friend, or a very good friend, once said, "If I ever met a gay person I would try to either kill him or run away." Which was a completely insane comment, he would never do any of those things, but there was a kind of crazy fear of gays and lesbians.

So just the experience of coming out and having people obviously not walk away, but in fact want to walk with me in that process. It was a process of really feeling loved and cared for, and that was just huge, that that was the response of the church that I encountered rather than harassment. And so mostly I experienced it as a privilege. To be in dialogue with [others]. And there were some decisions. I was actually dating a guy at the time, but I also knew that if I pursued a relationship with him that would be profoundly alienating for my family, and that mattered in some sense. And also it just seemed like the community was its own kind of adventure. It wasn't a choice between all the goodness of romantic love and a bleak life. It was a choice between two possible adventures.

ET: Has greater cultural acceptance [of homosexuality] made it harder for you in some ways?

TO: Living in San Francisco, the challenge for me is to be out as *celibate*. It honestly takes more courage than I often have, especially since I'm not entirely convinced of the Church's stance against same-sex marriage. But I am convinced that celibacy is its own worthwhile vocation in the context of the Church. And so if nothing else, I'm glad to live that out.

At work it seems like relationships and people's sexuality is such a topic of conversation, and so it's just a challenge for me to, first of all, be honest. Be honest that I'm gay, and if I admit that then they definitely want to know if I have a partner, and if I go on to say that actually I've committed myself to celibacy, then it seems like there's all sorts of judgments about my being repressed and a religious fanatic. All of those implicit judgments just seem very close to the surface. I feel like I can talk people through that, but that just takes a lot of energy and courage and so a lot of times I just don't open up any of that.

ET: Would you say that you had a "call to celibacy," or
is celibacy more like a consequence of another aspect of
your vocation—like, you had a call to this community,
and celibacy is part of what that means?

TO: Definitely the latter. I may just be projecting my own
experience on everybody else here, but it seems to me
that we're all made for partnership, and there's a huge
longing in each of us for that. I still [feel that] very much.

I think one of the good things of living in community
is seeing a lot of marriages up close, and seeing that even
if marriage is a great good, it's not salvation. There's that
passage in 1 Corinthians 7 where Paul talks about how
some have one gift and others another, and, at least in
Protestant circles, that often gets interpreted to mean that
to be celibate you have to have a special calling; you have
to have a certain gift; and I think that's a misinterpreta-
tion. I think Paul's not using gift in the sense of a spiritual
gift, but the more ordinary sense of something we might
give one another.

That's why I took a vow of celibacy: I hadn't been
receiving it as the potential gift it is. [So] I wanted to mine
this for the good that's in it, rather than continue to lust
after what I don't have.

I feel like I continued to have a fantasy life of, "Well,
if I met the perfect guy maybe I could move to a different
community that affirms same-sex relationships." I just felt
like I needed to put it to rest.

And so I called some friends and family and we had
about one-hundred people gather at a local church. I said
some vows and afterwards we had dinner and a dance,
and it ended up being a day where I felt really, really
loved. And prior to doing it, I had had a lot of agony

about, "Am I just being a complete drama queen here? Am I being self-absorbed? Am I making a big deal out of something which should be a quiet thing that I do in relation to God?" And maybe this is just self-justification in retrospect, but I really don't feel that. I feel that [the vow and ceremony] has put to rest some of those fantasies and discontent. I feel like I'm in a radically different phase. I know what my life is about and what I'm doing.

A lot of [the vows] came from the prayer of abandonment to divine providence.[1] And then I looked at some marriage vows and stole some things from them. I tried to emphasize that I felt like I was doing this in the context of community. I felt incredibly encouraged by the community and the kind of vow I took [was communal], like in a wedding, "We agree to . . ." I tried to do some of that stuff in the vows.

ET: What would you say to someone who thought they might be called to this kind of life? What would you say are some common misconceptions, including ones you had?

TO: The terrific thing is that I think there's ways of trying it short-term that kind of give you a taste, and a lot of communities have set up short-term opportunities to live in community. Part of that is a discernment process.

There's a terrific book that just came out by David Janzen, *The Intentional Christian Community Handbook*. There's a website called *Community of Communities*[2] that lists communities all over the US. But part of community is a trust that God works, the Spirit is especially present in God's people gathered, and so if someone is considering it I would encourage them to just pull together their own group of friends and have some discussions about it. "Do you see me as the kind of person who might do well in community?"

Experimentation is good, but also not necessarily reinventing the wheel. I don't particularly recommend, say, if you know three other people who are your same age, moving in together to do community. I feel like what happens is usually someone gets a job and moves away, and somebody else gets married, and that's painful and it more often than not comes to nothing and even leaves a bad taste in the people who survived. And so I would encourage people to find more established communities. Many Catholic orders have ways for laypeople to be [involved, for example] a third order. You might even end up with your three friends moving into a house, but I think that's much more likely to be good and worthwhile if you gleaned wisdom from people who have been doing it for a while.

As a young person, it's easy to romanticize it and think, "I'm just going to move in and we're all going to be best friends forever!" I wasn't realistic about how hard it is. But part of maturity is realizing that it's exactly in the hard places that we're challenged to grow. The difficulty is the catalyst that presents the motivation to actually grow. In any good life there's going to be a lot of pain and difficulty. [The best thing is] just being aware of that up front and [not] freaking out when it happens. Being aware that it's precisely in the hardest places where God is often most at work.

Tim points to some of the common themes of this book: Every vocation will challenge you and stress you out, and leave you feeling like you're in over your head. It will reshape you in the way the ocean reshapes a curving, twisting rock formation—by wearing you down. But every vocation can also be an "adventure," a gift. The pains and the joys can't be separated, although there will be seasons in which one or the other predominates. And you can't do any of this alone, by sheer willpower. Tim's recognition of the need to seek out guidance from people who have done these things before us—the need for precedents, even when the precedents only form imperfect parallels with our own experience—is a big part of why I'm writing this book.

Else We Shall Parish: Community, Honesty, and Acceptance

What about those of us who aren't called to the intense communal life Tim describes? I mean, when you say "intentional community," I hear "arguments over whether the cats should go vegan." But even those of us allergic to too much togetherness find that our Christian lives are usually built on smaller-scale, lower-intensity commitments to community. A parish is, or can be, a community. Within your average overstuffed Catholic parish there may also be sub-communities like the young adults' ministry or the homeless ministry.

These communities can offer much-needed succor for gay and same-sex attracted Christians. They can serve a role analogous to that of the extended family: maybe not as close and intense as your relationship with Mom and Dad but still an inescapable source of both support and obligation.

Even these communities require a lot of tolerance in order to function. We have to learn to get along with people very different from ourselves: Edith thinks if you don't help out with the church bazaar you are probably a Communist, and Masha thinks the bazaar is an abdication of our Christian duty, since we should really be giving those cloisonné Diaper Genies to the poor instead

of selling them. A good parish will be a difficult parish. It won't
be a parish where we only spend time with those who resemble
us or agree with us. A good parish will have the wild diversity of
the saints—and I don't imagine St. Jerome, for example, playing
well with others.

Gay people need places where we can be honest and where
we can begin to come out to ourselves and to others in a space
that may be safer than our homes and families. And in our own
honesty, we can model Christian life for others. We can ask for
help, and we can give it. We, too, are part of the difficult diversity
of a good parish.

Gregg, an Orthodox Christian, wrote on his blog, "When our
parishes function as real places of honesty and openness, gay
individuals will be free to be known and loved by their parish for
the unique person that they are. Their talents, gifts, and abilities
will find their unique place within the parish. By being honest
about my own gay orientation I have witnessed the deep power
that can come from being loved for who I uniquely am."[3]

I too have seen coming out deepen honesty and love within
one's parish community. While some people argue that coming
out is an inherently selfish act, imposing your quest for self-understanding on others, the vast majority of my experience suggests that this is completely backward. In most cases, by coming
out we not only make it easier to ask for help with our own
struggles but actually help others understand and live the faith.

A friend of mine told the people he worked with in a small
church ministry that he was gay. To his surprise, they reacted by
telling him that he should find a nice boyfriend! He explained to
them that this wasn't the kind of "support" he wanted or needed.
Through his honesty—not only about his orientation but about
his chastity—he offered a deeply countercultural witness.

Our parishes as a whole can offer that same startling witness, if we let them. We can make them places of refuge. In a society that generally treats gay people as political game pieces, scapegoats, or sidekicks, wouldn't it be great if the churches were the place where gay people were treated as people called by God?

If priests or pastors include prayers for gays, lesbians, and those with same-sex attraction, for example, that sends a signal. (And it doesn't require assuming that everyone who experiences same-sex attraction "struggles" with it—or that everyone who experiences it self-identifies as "gay.") Parish or church schools can stock the libraries with books like Wesley Hill's *Washed and Waiting: Reflections on Christian Faithfulness and Homosexuality*, and some of the other books listed in appendix one. At assemblies or in any other context that makes sense, principals and teachers can make it clear that students of any sexual orientation are welcome; they can stand against both bullying and the often devastating isolation, the smothering silence and fear, which too many gay Christian teens experience. These things need to be said explicitly because, unfortunately, if they're not said most people will assume that gay or same-sex attracted people *aren't* welcome. Like it or not, that's the public image of Christianity, and that image won't change until we do.

One of the parish communities in which I've served a lot of time is my church's ministry to gay and lesbian Catholics and our families and friends. This ministry is not the easiest one to work with. We try to "meet people where they are." We don't require you to have a position on the Church's teaching before you attend. That means meetings can sometimes feel like trying to herd not just cats, but cats plus dogs plus ferrets plus that *one* person who's gotta be a badger.

But it also means that people who always thought celibacy destroyed the soul can get to know people whose souls are nurtured by fidelity to Church teaching. It means that people who might be antagonists if the subject were gay marriage can come together to reassure a mother whose son just came out to her—who is choking back tears as she asks what she did wrong and mourning because she believes her son is doomed to misery in both this life and the next. I've seen this solidarity and it's one of the most powerful things you can imagine.

At a retreat on LGBT Christian issues, one of the other participants said something that stuck with me: "Sexual wholeness is more a property of communities or churches than it is of individuals." When it isn't a property of *our* local Christian communities, why not, and how can we change that?

chapter eleven
Service and Solidarity

Service to the neighbor may also take on a shape very hard to fit into the limits and constraints of society—a love akin to what Daniel Day Williams has called Franciscan love or what Gene Outka has described in discussing love as self-sacrifice. Such a love, because it seeks its own no more than Christ did, breaks through all the normal forms of life in society. Free of all claims to power, privilege, and possession—free even of all desires except the one overmastering desire to follow Christ—this type of Christian lover goes out in search of his neighbor.

—Gilbert Meilaender,
Friendship: A Study in Theological Ethics, page 33

These are the corporal works of mercy (using the list from the online *Catholic Encyclopedia*):

- To feed the hungry;
- To give drink to the thirsty;
- To clothe the naked;
- To harbor the harborless;
- To visit the sick;
- To ransom the captive; and
- To bury the dead.

And these are the spiritual works of mercy:

- To instruct the ignorant;

- To counsel the doubtful;

- To admonish sinners;

- To bear wrongs patiently;

- To forgive offenses willingly;

- To comfort the afflicted; and

- To pray for the living and the dead.

Some of these sound more fun than others. Who wouldn't prefer instructing the ignorant to bearing wrongs patiently? Can we count adopting an adorable little stray kitten as "harboring the harborless"? That's totally comforting the afflicted too, right?

In reality, of course, most of us are not adorable when we're most in need. We are more like the mistrustful stray cat with a smelly infection and a tendency to bite and claw when she feels threatened. But it's precisely because the works of mercy can be tough that they can teach us how to love. Mercy stretches and challenges us. It exposes our own weaknesses—how easily we're annoyed by others' needs, for example—but also gives us the succor we need. In serving others we often begin to rebuild a sense of self shattered by addiction or sin; and by watching how other battered and scrawny cats begin to clean up we gain inspiration and role models for our own lives.

Every Christian life will require some of these works of mercy. But many of us also sense a special call to service. I knew that I wanted to start serving in some specific, required, and scheduled capacity when I moved back to DC. I learned a lot through serving as a crisis pregnancy counselor, and several of those lessons were pertinent to my life as a gay Catholic.

First of all, I learned that it's important to find one's *own* vocation. Know your call, and know your limits. Meredith has done hospice work, for example, which I'm pretty sure would be wrong for me. I'd feel overwhelmed, awkward, and frustrated, and therefore self-centered. By contrast, she knows that crisis pregnancy counseling isn't for her. "I'm already too cynical about men," she once noted. (This reminds me of the line from Dorothy Allison's essay, "Talking to Straight People": "There is no lesbian in the world that could hate men the way straight women do."[1])

I knew that I wanted to work with women. I didn't think too much about this element of my longing for service. I did think it was probably related in some complex way to my sexual orientation. The '70s lesbian feminists sometimes used the phrase "women's energies" to describe a certain distinctive rightness and belonging which is partly physical—the curve of a hip or a breast, the bright or husky tones of a woman's voice—and partly based on solidarity. I think that was a large part of what I wanted in service.

This isn't about sexual attraction at all—I have zero interest in sleeping with the women I counsel, and it would be a very troubling sign if that changed. It's a call that runs deeper, a longing that couldn't be filled by sex even if sex were an option. It's about connecting with other women on the basis, in part, of our shared womanhood.

Regularly loving and receiving love from women has refreshed my soul and helped me to see the injured beauty of God's creations. Crisis pregnancy counseling has allowed me to be what the Second Wave feminists called a "woman-identified woman" and a "woman-loving woman." Whatever else you might want to say about the Second Wave, they understood that many women have a profound need for connection with other women *as women*. I found that connection in large part through counseling.

This doesn't mean that every woman needs to work with women or needs to have a particularly strong feeling of connection to other women. One of the problems with the Second Wave "woman-identified woman" mindset was the way it led feminists to judge those with whom they disagreed as "male-identified"— treasonous women or not real women at all. I especially don't want to suggest that lesbians all have some kind of deficiency in our womanhood or our identification as women, which must be fixed by service to women. But for me, as someone whose lesbianism often played out as a desire to serve and care for my girlfriends, I did find that pregnancy counseling helped to fill a profound need I had to serve women.

A major benefit of this work is that it can be kind of messy. Kids poop, and kids projectile vomit. (When you least expect it!) Scared young women trying to take pregnancy tests find that their hands shake so much that they spill the cup of urine, and it's my job to clean it up and respond to their tearful apologies with tenderness and reassurance. I listed the corporal works of mercy first because they tend to be the more physical works of mercy, the ones where you wash dirty and swollen feet or chop giant piles of onions until your face is streaming with tears. We live in a weirdly anti-physical culture, a culture that fetishizes choice and will at the expense of the messy, recalcitrant, mute needs of the body. Like kneeling in prayer, kneeling to scrub a floor humbles us and reminds us that we serve God with our bodies as well as with our minds and desires.

For celibate gay Christians there may be an especial temptation to dissociate from our bodies. This isn't a temptation I've faced personally since my conversion, but I know many, many people who have struggled with feeling like the body is an enemy, a howling madman to whom their minds are shackled, or at best a distraction from their love for God and their good intentions. This is a source of misery, and it can become a rejection of God as Creator. Our bodies are created and sustained in every moment by God's love. We must find ways to honor his creation. The pain we suffer from desire is like the pain Christ suffered—the thorn in the flesh, like the thorns with which he was crowned. And the remedy for this pain is neither to ignore it nor to scold and speak firmly to our pain and hope it obeys the rational voice of the mind. Other and better ways to approach any rejection or disgust we feel toward our bodies and desires include praying and welcoming God into the midst of our troubled hearts and flesh. He never disdains to be with us. He is never disgusted by our desires. We can also find ways to find joy and solace in our bodies. Reception of the Eucharist and eucharistic adoration may help us focus on God specifically in his *Incarnation*, in his flesh. Kneeling in prayer, walking in a garden, playing with your dog—all of these are graces of the body, gifts of the body, and our joy and gratitude in these experiences are themselves a kind of prayer.

So too, service that uses the body as much as the mind (realizing, of course, that this is an artificial and unreal distinction) can be a way of accepting that bodies are weird, bodies are needy, and that's all right. That's how we were made.

Our bodies, like our souls, were made for love.

Working with women in crisis pregnancies had one totally unexpected benefit for me: it helped me to understand, on a visceral level, the crosses and sacrifices specific to *heterosexuality*. I don't think there's any point in lecturing people about how "we all have our crosses, so stop whining," but working at the pregnancy center helped me see how much the Christian faith asks of men who want to sleep with women, and women who want to sleep with men. It has helped me understand that while gay Catholics do face unique and intensely painful challenges, the same is true for straight Christians—and in the case of poor women, especially, those challenges are ignored and disrespected just as much as ours are. The women we served were shamed and stigmatized for, in many cases, *good* decisions they had made as well as bad. At a gay youth group, I met teens whose parents had threatened to throw them out of the house if they were gay. At the pregnancy center, I met teens whose parents had threatened to throw them out of the house if they didn't get an abortion.

Working with women, mostly Christian women, facing crisis pregnancies helped me feel sympathy and solidarity with straight people and made it harder for me to be bitter and resentful about my own situation. These women were also able to challenge and inspire me. I saw women make decisions that would damage their economic prospects, their marriage prospects, their relationship with their parents, their self-image, and their reputation in order to give a child life and obey God.

Poor women who become pregnant out of wedlock are intensely stigmatized, and one of our biggest tasks at the center is helping women see the life inside them as something more than a source of shame. Seeing women face down their shame in order to serve Christ has been deeply convicting for me. It's helped me immensely in dealing with the various stigmas and shames which come with being gay—and with being celibate for religious reasons, which carries its own stigma in many circles. I've never been ashamed of being gay that I can recall, but there have been many times when the frequent small, grinding humiliations of explaining my celibacy left me feeling worn down, resentful, and equal parts self-righteous and ashamed.

But at the center, being celibate was an opportunity. Not necessarily in the way you might expect. I don't think I've ever talked about my sexual orientation with a client who wasn't herself gay or bisexual, and even with gay or bi clients (we do see them), I haven't always shared my personal situation if it seemed distracting or inappropriate. So I don't say, "Well, I know something about abstinence myself! You see . . ." My situation is very different from that of a woman who does hope to marry a man one day, and besides, frankly, the weirdness of getting crisis pregnancy counseling from a celibate lesbian would be a distraction from the client's needs. My job is to serve her needs, not to "share my story" or some such self-centered idea.

Celibacy, as I have lived it for ten years so far, brings an entirely different benefit: It makes you able to offer hospitality on the fly. One benefit of priestly celibacy in the Western Church is that it makes priests radically *available* to pour themselves out for God and their parish, without the responsibilities of a married man with kids. Similarly, when I was living on my own, I was able to offer homeless women a place to stay while we found them better housing. I could make that decision spontaneously, responding only to the client's needs, without having to consult anyone else. The radical vulnerability of celibate laypeople can free us to help those even more vulnerable than ourselves.

Hospitality can be tiring. Radical hospitality can be exhausting. But it is a gift many celibate lay people can give.

Service to others can be one way for celibates to "be fruitful." Most of us are called to serve the next generation by becoming parents; for the rest of us, something like pregnancy center work may be one way for our loving service to last beyond our own deaths. We can leave a legacy. When I've gone on to sing off-key in the Choir Invisible, there will be people in the world who might not be there if God hadn't allowed me to help their mothers choose life. That's a pretty powerful reminder that fruitfulness goes beyond procreation.

Families as Sites of Service

In both this chapter and the preceding one, I've written as if we go out and find a community to live within or serve. That's true for many people. But it's also an overly individualist model of vocation. Vocational discernment can become its own form of navel-gazing, its own emerging-adulthood identity quest, in which we ignore the people among whom God has placed us and go out seeking for a more congenial group of people to serve. Sometimes nobody's as hard to love as your own family.

For many gay people, the family is an especially fraught site where we've suffered intense and even violent rejection. That's one reason I do want to emphasize the many other paths to a loving and fruitful life. But if you can serve your family of origin—if they'll let you care for them without tormenting you—maybe that's what God is calling you to do.

This used to be fairly normal: the sisters or brothers who lived together all their lives or the beloved aunt who shared the family home. As worldwide demographics shift, we'll see more people caring for aging parents, as well. Researcher Dorothy A. Miller coined the term "sandwich generation," for the adults caught between the demands of young children and their own elderly parents, but it can feel less like a sandwich and more like that garbage-crushing room in *Star Wars*. If you can wedge yourself between the walls, easing the burdens of either childcare, elder care, or both, you will be doing a true work of mercy.

This is a countercultural suggestion. We've been trained to think of adulthood as a process of leaving the family home. "Returning to the nest" is the nice way to put it, but the not nice ways include terms like "failure to launch." Adults who live with their families of origin are often stigmatized as failures, manchildren and womanchildren who can't do their own laundry or hold down a job. And yet for many families, an adult's need to love, sacrifice, and serve can meet a parent's or sibling's needs to be cared for and helped. There may be significant financial savings for the family, but even if not, the adult's willingness to take on the task of caring for his or her kin should be praised, not shamed.

chapter twelve
Challenges Within Your Vocation

Before people are married in the Church, they receive marriage counseling; while the quality of this counseling may vary from location to location, the structure for formation is there. Similarly, when someone joins a religious order, they have to undergo intensive formation before becoming a full member; again, the quality of formation will vary widely, but the structure is there. But it seems safe to say that, as a rule (though particular circumstances may make it untrue in concrete situations), the person who lives celibacy in the world has, in her or his life, the least and frailest support structures of all; yet he or she is expected to live chastity with the most general guidance and the fewest concrete examples.

—Joshua Gonnerman,
"Some Tools of Chaste Living," spiritualfriendship.org

The title of this chapter should be self-explanatory: These are common problems that can crop up in your life even if you have discerned and are trying to carry out your vocation. I'll suggest remedies that I or other people have found helpful. These suggestions won't always help. We are never alone, but there will be times when we feel alone. This book is about making those times less frequent and more survivable.

(Sometimes You Want to Go) Where Nobody Knows Your Name

The worst thing about celibacy for me has been the lack of accountability. You come home, and there's nobody there. (At my old apartment, I couldn't even have a cat!) It was easy to feel like nobody would know or care what I did except God, and maybe God would blink. Obviously, this feeling of not being *watched*—no lifeguard on duty, swim at your own risk—played a role in my alcoholism. It's not at all surprising to me that, although we all know of couples whose addiction develops in tandem and who drag each other down, overall marriage is correlated with a lower risk of addiction. Celibate people lack that protection.

You can seek out accountability if you find that you need it. (Catholics will need to be going to confession anyway.) I found that one of my most pressing needs was a regular confessor, so I couldn't "shop around" to find someone who wouldn't remember me and remember that I had a drinking problem. People whose churches don't practice individual confession may still be able to find what are sometimes called "accountability partners." I've known several especially sincere Americans who have been able to explicitly ask their friends to hold them accountable—to call them out when they seem to be lying to themselves or haring off in a bad moral direction. This works for them, and has deepened their friendships as well. It's a little *too* American for me, a little too close to the thing where you're just trying to buy laundry detergent, but the clerk wants to know if you've accepted Jesus into your heart. But if it sounds good to you and your friends, I can tell you that many people get a lot from creating a kind of mini-community of accountability.

I've found accountability primarily through practicing much greater honesty and vulnerability in my friendships than I'm comfortable with, and through spiritual direction with a priest I trust. Meredith knows that I sometimes need to be prodded to talk about my feelings and girly crap like that, and she's willing to check up on me and even guilt-trip me into being honest with her. Just knowing that she's aware of my various anxieties makes them easier to talk about and makes me more aware of my own duplicity and denial when I try to hide them from her.

I've also, of course, gotten a huge boost in this area from living with my family. If you and your family can stand one another this might be a surprisingly good, countercultural way to make a fruitful life for yourself. I'm pretty firmly opposed to the bizarre capitalism-versus-the-family mindset in which living with your parents as an adult makes you a manchild or woman-child. It might make you someone who not only acknowledges her weaknesses but has figured out a way to shore up her weak points while looking after others.

Prayers to St. Joan of Arc

I feel very lucky to have entered the Church with a high level of anti-clericalism and cynicism about the clergy. When bishops do something right for once I can be grateful, and when they act like bureaucrats at best, I am not surprised.

Nonetheless, I've experienced the anger and resentment toward the Church and its representatives that most gay Christians grapple with at some point. I've been furious with bishops who say dumb things about gay people, and felt intense frustration with Catholic leaders who stand in the way of efforts to reach out to gay young people.

Much of this anger is justified. I know people who have been denied jobs by Catholic institutions because they are open about their sexual orientation—and also open about their fidelity to Church teaching on chastity. The Catechism prohibits "unjust discrimination" against people who are same-sex attracted; if that language covers anything, I think it covers firing someone for telling you why he's celibate. Moreover, Catholic schools and dioceses typically have no programs or guidance for gay teens.

There's just so much callousness—often provoked by fear—and so much wincing hypercaution. And meanwhile kids are killing themselves because of our silence and indifference. Anger can sometimes fuel our passion for justice; it can give us the urgency we need to overcome our own fears and exhaustion.

The problem is that even a clean anger so easily becomes a kind of infected, resentful anger, which can't solve any of the problems that caused it. *It doesn't matter that you're right.* Some of your best qualities—a hunger for justice, solidarity with other queer people, fidelity to Church teaching, a feeling of belonging to and love for the Church—can be twisted into sources of wrath, judging, and other serious sins.

The first remedy is one I found on a bumper sticker. It was sold by a Catholic blog called *Disputations*, and it just said, "Have you tried prayer and fasting?" Nothing's more practical. I'd specifically suggest prayer to saints who clashed with the Church authorities of their time—of whom Joan of Arc may be the most dramatic representative. St. Catherine of Siena, who rebuked the pope, is another good choice. (I note that both of these saints are women. G.W.F. Hegel's line that woman is "the irony of the community" applies just as much to the Catholic Church as elsewhere.)

The other remedy I've found may need some tweaking to be relevant to you: when I'm angry, I listen to disco. The bishops put out some kind of statement on homosexuality, asymptotically approaching understanding at the speed of a dying snail, and I throw on a Pet Shop Boys album. There's a certain exhilarating beauty, an antigravity feeling, to great disco. For you it may be some other form of art or experience of beauty that lifts your spirits and shakes you free of the heavy emotions of anger, resentment, and self-righteousness.

The goal here is not to distract you from your purpose or scold you for feeling angry. The goal is to renew your spirit so that you can witness to the truth with love rather than resentment.

The Bible gives us examples of faithful people bringing their anger to God. You can talk to him however you want and with whatever you actually feel; you don't have to polish up your emotional state before you pray. He has already heard Abraham's lawyering, Sarah's laughter, Job's misery, and much more.

Falling in Love Is So Hard on the Knees

Falling in love is one of the worst things that could happen to a gay person, because you will necessarily be heartbroken, you will have to run away, and that will happen every single time that you come to care about someone else too much. [1]

That's Matthew Vines's depiction, in a popular YouTube video, of how life looks from the orthodox Christian perspective. It's a poignant, powerful statement. And I've seen it play out in some of my friends' lives. There are times when falling in love *can* seem like a catastrophe, as if you've betrayed God or he's betrayed you.

This isn't the best way to look at things. Would we say that "the worst thing that can happen" to a celibate priest is that he falls in love, or summarize the plot of *Brief Encounter* as "the worst thing that can happen to a married woman is falling in love"? But there's enough truth in Vines' words for them to sting.

Crushes—I'm using this word to mean the kind of new, heady, burning love that can sometimes be transformed into a deeper and more mature love—present painful challenges to celibate gay people. It's especially hard when you have a crush on a friend, maybe even someone whose friendship you have relied on for support precisely in times of religious crisis.

There's no obvious "answer" here. For me, sometimes crushes have been transformed into mature friendships. I can express my love in that way and be happy. I get to laugh with and care for a beautiful woman—how should I complain? But I realize that I'm unusually attuned to modes of sublimation.

Some friends of mine have needed a difficult period of separation from their friend/crush. Some found that the friendship never fully recovered. For all of these people the friendship truly was, as St. Aelred suggested all of our deepest friendships can be, an occasion of the Cross. They had to die to self. These wounds of love heal only with time, if they heal at all.

Time—including time apart, if being with the person you have a crush on is damaging your faith or your sense of who you are—and prayer, confession, and honesty with your other friends (unless that honesty would require you to reveal too much about your crush, in which case you should seek out someone who isn't involved, like a spiritual director or accountability partner). Those are the only remedies I can think of. I will tell you that everyone I've just described, who did not give up on Christian orthodoxy in these different but equally painful situations, now has a stronger relationship with Christ than they did before they were challenged in this way. Their relationship with God is perhaps chastened now in a way it wasn't before—the marriage in *Brief Encounter* ends up stronger by the end of the movie but also sadder, with a tenderness born from acceptance of pain.

A crush on a friend may be an opportunity to strengthen your other friendships. It can certainly deepen your friendship with God.

Economic Consequences of Celibacy

I joked that this section would just be one line: "You may end up living with your parents." But actually there are negative economic effects of lay celibacy, for the same reasons there are positive economic effects of marriage. You're nagged less, which means you take worse care of yourself and don't work as hard. You have fewer demands on your time, perhaps, but also fewer incentives to push yourself in your profession. You may be less stable (I obviously know something about that) and that will affect your wallet as well. You can't pool costs as well, and you can't specialize: If something needs to be done in your life, you will probably be the one doing it, even if you're not that good at it. This may be terrific if it means you learn to cook, or to snake a pipe (is that a thing? I'm just making up terms now so I sound competent), but it can also mean you live less efficiently and less comfortably. These little life challenges can wear you down, and even damage your health and resilience. Remember to ask for help when you can.

And there can be bigger consequences to celibacy if you don't have *somebody* watching your back. We all need someone who sees our emergencies as their emergencies too. Brent Bailey, who blogs about his gay Christian life at *Odd Man Out*, wrote:

> One of the ways in which many Christians in our particular setting have failed to exercise their imaginations, I think, is in our concept of the family. We've perceived benefits of the heterosexual nuclear family structure to the degree that we no longer imagine healthy and satisfying relationships outside of that formal structure, and we're unconscious of the way *Jesus initiated a new family paradigm that was an absolute economic and*

social necessity for many of the people who left brothers or sisters or mother or father or children to follow him.[2]

If we Christians are brothers and sisters to one another, we need to care for each other like family—and that means economic support as well as emotional support. The early church knew that those who had sacrificed respectable family life for Christ needed a new family *in* Christ. Today, that might look like several unmarried laypeople living together as friends. It might look like a godparent living with the godchild's family, becoming an honorary uncle or aunt. It might look like an adult living with his parents, offering mutual support. All of these arrangements are both emotionally healthier and more economically sustainable than a parish of singletons waiting to be eaten by their cats.

You're Never All the Way Out

I think many straight people underestimate how much time and mental energy a lot of gay people spend figuring out when and whether to come out. You don't want to bring up personal matters unnecessarily or start a potentially difficult conversation with someone you don't know well; and yet it can seem even trickier and more weighted to come out later, when you've gotten to know a person who nonetheless has made a fairly important wrong assumption about you. There are the moments when people start making blithe comments about "those people" and there are the questions about your future and your relationships, which you'd like to be able to answer forthrightly and yet always feel like you're hedging or hiding something. I'm out to *the world*; I'm basically a professional homosexual at this point, and my sexual orientation and my faith are pretty much the first things you learn about me if you Google my name—and I still end up going through a lot of internal drama about when and how to come out to new people. New housemates, new people at my volunteer job, or friends of friends. Straight Christians often assume that our sexual orientation is rarely relevant, when in fact it generally comes up in even casual relationships if they last long enough. And then people want to know why you didn't mention it earlier.

This goes double if you're celibate for religious reasons. Now you add to "I'm gay," which can be jarring, "and I'm also a thing of which you probably don't know any other examples." People who don't have unpleasant stereotypes about or condescending reactions to gay people in general may have them about celibate gay people: *Oh, you poor thing! Why would you do that to yourself? Why don't you just become an Episcopalian? That's so creepy (or harmful or self-deceiving); you must hate yourself. It's just a phase. What a waste!* Or, if you're in a traditional Christian environment where people are trying to be very tolerant and kind, you may get blank looks followed by, *You're so brave!*

All of this is minor but can feel tiring and bruising. I don't think there really is a solution other than to accept that coming out can be awkward, but it often improves relationships once the initial awkwardness is past. Recognize that every single one of us is stereotyped and judged—this is one of the joys of life in a globalized society—and try to have friends you can commiserate with. Pray for the ability to see yourself through God's eyes, not through the eyes of the people around you.

Representative Hypocrisy

Once you've done the coming-out thing, a whole new kind of problem opens up for you. Some people will be serious when they say that you're brave. They will think of you as practically a martyr for the faith, someone leading an incredible, saintly Christian life. Or they may think of you as, if not admirable,

at least kind of extra-Christian. If they're not Christian themselves, you may be someone they consider a representative of
the faith.

No pressure!

One thing I've found particularly hard to deal with is the gap
between the public image of the Celibate Gay Christian and the
messy reality of my life. It can feel like you're carrying on your
shoulders the weight of *everybody's* expectations of your group.
As I put it to my first spiritual director, "Imagine if you were the
only Catholic priest anybody ever met."

The shame I felt over the gap between my public image
and my private self was part of what made it so hard for me
to get help and stop drinking. Even if your problems aren't as
flamboyant as that, you still need people who can let you be
flawed, who can let you be a normal sinner—people who won't
read way too much into your every doubt, sin, or speculative
comment.

The best approach to take here will depend on your personality. I've seen people do very well by crafting a kind of knock-
about, "everybody knows I'm crazy" persona, and fitting your
Christianity into that can take some of the pressure off. If you're
clear enough that you're a weird old mess, it's harder to turn you
into some kind of representative Christian.

If your natural personality is more reserved or you tend
toward a more sincere emotional style, having a couple of close
friends you can confide in is especially important—people who
see you as yourself, not as a photo caption.

Good news: This problem will diminish as more celibate
gay Christians come out. The more examples there are, the less
any one person has to be an example. As we make our mistakes, argue with each other, and model radically different

ways of serving God, it will become obvious that none of us is representative.

Amateur Dramatics

If you've been intensely unhappy or anxious about the intersection of your sexuality and your faith for a long time, your mind has gotten used to that anxiety. Depressed and dramatic feels normal. When you start to experience peace and trust in God, it can be profoundly unsettling for your mind and spirit. You may find yourself getting ridiculously anxious about tiny things or creating problems for yourself by stirring up drama among your friends. These are ways to recreate the stress you're used to. Stress is exciting, in a way, but more than that, it feels like *home* to you in a way that peace doesn't.

If you find yourself acting this way, point it out to yourself and laugh about it. Out of the frying pan, into the . . . wait, why are you setting a fire?!

But also, try focusing on God's forgiveness. Try seeing your behavior as God would see it: not with judgmental eyes but with tender (and maybe slightly bemused) eyes. Remind yourself that you are being held in his hands and carried, and you can trust in that even when you know you can't trust your own strength.

Apologize when you need to. Accept that you may have a well-deserved reputation as a drama magnet. And remember (this is what I struggle with) that apologies don't fix things immediately. The only thing that will rebuild your friendships and give greater peace to your soul is time.

Sex and Shame

Compulsive sexual activity isn't just a "celibate" problem or a "gay" problem. Plenty of husbands will tell you that marriage doesn't cure the ache or the overwhelming urge, and it can even deepen what might seem an already impossibly intense shame. Anonymous or emotionally disconnected sex may be much more available to gay men than to anybody else because of various unfortunate collisions of male biology and cultural conditioning, but men and women in every walk of life find themselves caught in this depressing, depleting cycle.

My own thoughts here are pretty limited. Try to find a compassionate counselor or spiritual director who leaves you feeling hope rather than discouragement. My own spiritual director told me, "Discouragement is always from the devil," which is some of the wisest advice I know. Do all the things you should be doing anyway in terms of prayer and basic self-care, like eating right and trying to stay on a regular schedule—all the boring stuff which makes a much bigger difference than I used to think. Try to minimize the danger—physical and emotional—to yourself and others, even if you can't get your life entirely in order. When Jesus told the rich young man to sell all that he had and give to the poor, the young man didn't do it. But that doesn't mean his life of virtue, his following of the commandments, was simply meaningless. His goodness wasn't canceled out by his recalcitrance. If you're working with homeless sick people in the early evening and then going out to find a man behind the monuments, yeah, that obviously isn't the life God wants for you as I'm sure you already know, but it's not a worthless life; there's a great deal of good in it.

And life isn't a step-by-step process where doing the right stuff gets you the right outcome. It's not a Play-Doh Fun Factory where you can put the shapeless dough of human misery in one end and get perfectly coiled spaghetti out the other. There will be times when nothing helps and you just need to hang on. Try to remember that you're being sheltered in Christ's wounds, where he keeps those who are closest to him. Keep St. Paul's words in

mind: "Therefore, that I might not become too elated, a thorn in
the flesh was given to me, an angel of Satan, to beat me, to keep
me from being too elated. Three times I begged the Lord about
this, that it might leave me, but he said to me, 'My grace is sufficient for you, for power is made perfect in weakness.' I will rather
boast most gladly of my weaknesses, in order that the power of
Christ may dwell with me" (2 Cor 12:7–9).

Paul may be referring to a besetting sin or temptation, or to
physical suffering, or even, some suggest, to a difficult person
among the flock. But many people have found his words especially applicable to recurring sins and temptations; the humiliation of falling in the same way, yet again, is a powerful cure for
vanity and a reminder of our total dependence on God. In this
way, even our sins can become a channel for God's grace.

And whatever Paul meant, there is at least one saint who
did not receive release from his burden of compulsive sin and
shame. Heather King, a Catholic writer and recovering alcoholic, was startled and gratified to learn of the life of St. Mark
Ji Tianxiang:

> A friend of mine recently sent me an unusual holy card. It hon-
> ors St. Mark Ji Tianxiang, a Chinese layman who was murdered
> in 1900, along with dozens of other Catholics in his village, in
> the vicious persecution of Christians during the Boxer rebellion.
> That's not the unusual thing. The Church has canonized many
> martyrs, including many Chinese martyrs. What's unusual
> about St. Mark is that he was an opium addict who was barred
> from receiving the sacraments for the last 30 years of his life.
>
> Mark couldn't receive communion because his addiction
> was regarded as gravely sinful and scandalous. He prayed for
> deliverance from his addiction, but deliverance never came.
> Nevertheless, he remained a believing Catholic. At his trial,
> he was given a chance to renounce his faith, but he refused. It

is said that he sang the litany of the Blessed Virgin Mary as he was led to his execution.

Saints are exemplary people. The Church creates them so we can learn from them. So what can we learn from St. Mark Ji Tianxiang?

For starters, he shows that anybody can become a saint— even a man who was kicked out of the church for giving public scandal. By canonizing him, the Church also signals a different attitude toward addiction than the one St. Mark's pastors had a century ago. Drug abuse is sinful, but addiction is also a disease of the mind and body. Addicts today are not excluded from the sacraments because they are addicts.

I also marvel at St. Mark's confidence in the mercy of God. He probably shared the village's opinion of him—that he was serious sinner who was behaving terribly. He must have felt despair in his futile struggles and perhaps some bitterness too. But he persevered in his faith. I suspect that in his brokenness he met the suffering Christ. In the end, he went to his death confidently, trusting that love would receive him. May we all imitate St. Mark.[3]

How does God view such people? Well, the Church views at least one of them as a saint, so that's a hint. And we can also see a hint if we return to the story of the rich young man. When Jesus encounters this man, Mark tells us that right before Jesus tells him to give up his possessions, "Jesus, looking at him, loved him." (Mk 10:21) The most important thing about your life isn't its secret shames, even though that's often how we feel. And the most important verdict on your life isn't your own. The way your life looks *objectively* is the way it looks to God: the life of his beloved child. Try to picture yourself, right now, through God's eyes. Try to see yourself with the eyes of love. Then remove everything from that image that discourages you: the disappointment you may be imagining, or the "yes, I love you, but" sorrow,

or the stern "tough love" glare. When all of that is gone, what is
left is clear and steady, a look that gazes directly into your eyes
rather than looking down on you. That is the God who knows
you, understands you, and loves you even—especially—when
you are least capable of loving yourself. That is the Christian God.

When I was trying, unsuccessfully, to quit drinking, I had
one night in a hotel room when I was praying pretty intensely
and making real progress, albeit haltingly. I managed to call up
images of some of the most humiliating things I'd done—not
the *worst* things, not the unkindness and selfishness, which we
somehow usually manage to repent without really loathing, but
the most shameful things—and invite God into those moments.
I imagined him there, as in fact he was there, seeing it all and
not turning away from me. I "invited" him, the way you have
to invite a vampire in—you have to invite God into your heart
and your memory in the same way if you want forgiveness. It
was ridiculously painful and to this day, I can't do it most of the
time, but it was also one of the closest encounters I've ever had
with the truth about the shocking completeness of God's mercy.

And then I got back from my business trip and bought a
comfortingly large bottle of Smirnoff, you know? Mercy and penitence don't always "work"; they are sufficient in themselves and
have no other "point" or purpose. Still, denying yourself mercy
will pretty much always make your life worse. Mary Karr got it
right when she said, "That schoolmarm part of me—that hyper-
critical finger-wagging part of myself that I thought was gonna
keep me sober—that is actually what helped me stay drunk. What
keeps you sober is love and connection to something bigger than
yourself."[4]

To Come First for Someone

I think a lot of gay celibate people have enormous anxiety that our singleness means we face the world alone. We have nobody to consider our emergencies *their* emergencies, nobody who will always be there for us. We phrase it in different ways. One man poignantly asked me about the longing "to come *first* for someone." Here's my response:

There are a lot of pieces to this emotion. To be always the one who watches the love between spouses or parents and children, supporting that intense your-needs-first love but never receiving it yourself. Never knowing that there's somebody who will always take your call. Asking yourself who your emergency contact should be, rather than filling in the name without thinking about it. Feeling like you're burdening people when you need them—like you're asking them to do something outrageously above and beyond the call of duty when you ask them to sacrifice time, effort, or their own priorities to care for you, even when you're really seriously in need.

And I think there are at least four things to say to this poignant longing. Let me move from the most abstract to the most personal.

First, the whole ideal of "coming first" for someone all the time, and marriage as the institution that provides that to the spouses, would sound really weird to 99.99 percent of people who have ever lived. Going into marriage expecting that now you have found "your person," who will always be there for you, who will always come first for you, and for whom you will always come first, is a setup for intense disappointment and pain. Seriously, imagine describing marriage like this to a woman in any century before the twentieth; I doubt you could find even a handful who'd know what the heck you were talking about.

And not always for bad reasons—often the children will come first. In a Christian marriage, God should always come first, and that has real consequences for how you feel about your spouse's decisions. There's a probably apocryphal (attributed to several other saints) story about my confirmation saint, St. Elizabeth of Hungary, in which she blurted out a lie to her husband so she could keep spending their wealth on feeding the poor, and God chose to turn her lie into the truth. Her husband, who in this story later became a deeply devout man himself, came approximately third for her during that time in their marriage: God first, then the poor, and eventually her husband. And this story was part of her legend, part of the lessons her life could teach Christians.

So "coming first for someone" isn't necessarily something heterosexuals should be asking of their marriages, let alone something we should envy them for. It comes close to the Western mistake of turning marriage into *folie à deux*.

That said, everybody rightly longs to give and receive sacrificial love—and by "sacrificial love" I mean soup when you're sick, a compassionate ear when you're lonely, a shoulder when you cry, and a sense that you matter intensely to others. A sense that your needs aren't hideous intrusions into other people's lives but part of the work of love. This is an area where our refusal to honor or even imagine important vocations other than marriage causes a huge amount of pain, loneliness, and sense of worthlessness. If we took friendship seriously as a potential site of devotion and sacrifice, far fewer people would feel neglected and unwanted. If we considered lay community life ("intentional communities") more seriously, and if we expanded our concept of family and welcomed single people into familial homes (for a season or for life), many more people could have the experience of living in a realistic familial love in which we all come first at times, and nobody is just there as support personnel. People in these vocations would still have problems, since devoted friend-ship, community, and family aren't easy, but they'd be better problems.

I do think cultural changes would ease some of the loneliness and uncertainty about one's worth that I think are embedded in this desire to come first for someone. But it's important to go beyond cultural criticism. Because we do come first for some-body: we come first for Christ. And there will be times when we need to rely on his love alone. If you'd be ready to work on a marriage, consider working on your relationship with Christ. We are cherished and adored by him, he will always "take our calls," and I don't think I need to tell you that he's willing to sacrifice for us. The most realistic and practical prescription for cultural change and personal longing for love is always Christ.

And finally, maybe the most important thing to say about this desire to "come first" is simply that I've felt it too. It's been really hard for me sometimes. Other times, like now, I don't feel it as strongly. But maybe the most important thing I can offer in response to this painful and pretty humbling cry isn't advice or theology but just solidarity. I feel it too.[5]

Another celibate gay blogger put it this way in a post called "Wanted for Possession":

> There was a fairly long period of my life where one thought in particular would almost bring me to tears whenever it crossed my mind. "You know, Jordan, if everyone in the world paired up, nobody would choose you. You'd be all alone. Alone. Alone. Alone. Alone . . ."
>
> My subconscious was like a tool that had discovered a reverb machine.
>
> It was only recently that I finally discerned what exactly was going on for those two or three years: I was craving exclu-sivity. In the throes of a crippling fear of a dark and lonely future, I felt, viscerally and relentlessly, that if I just had one

person, *one person* who I knew would choose me above anybody then I would have peace and all would be well. It might also end world poverty! (I was a desperate prayer-bargainer). This made me a terribly jealous friend. I knew it was bad, I knew I was ruining my ability to be content in my relationships, but I didn't know how to stop that panicky ache from flaring up. . . .

Sexuality is never about possessing someone. Never. It is, rather, *all* about giving yourself to another. And not just *one* other. We serve a Christ who has literally given himself entirely for the sake of *everyone.* . . .

Once I began opening up to people, abandoning my desperate quest for exclusivity, the loneliness, the anxiety, and the fear began to dissipate like an unwelcome morning haze. It was only when I stopped trying to possess my friends that I actually felt secure in my friendships. And on top of that, I was finding increasing joy in my interactions with almost everyone because I was persistently asking myself how I could be used to bless them, to communicate to them their immense worth before God. I need to be careful not to over-do it, as always, being sure to pace myself so I don't bleed out on the altar of self-giving. But thus far, it has only been a fantastic turn of events in my life.

This is what sexuality, properly oriented, is designed to do—it draws us to others so that we might display to them the love of God and receive from them the same.[6]

I love this post because it describes how the hunger for exclusivity or "first-ness" not only flows out of loneliness but exacerbates it. And loneliness itself is our next and final stop on this tour of common difficulties faced by celibate gay people.

Lonely Hearts Club

For me the loneliness of celibacy hasn't primarily been about wanting to be physically around other people. I enjoy my own company, and I see my friends and family pretty frequently. The difficulty comes more when I feel overextended: when I feel like there's nobody with the time or interest to listen to my problems, when the people I'd ordinarily rely on are busy with their own relationships and worries, and when I'm working hard to be there for others emotionally but have to recognize that they're not able to be there for me right now.

This is one excellent reason to make more friends—and be more honest with them. But to a certain extent this kind of loneliness is just something you have to accept. If it helps, it does happen to spouses and parents too. The man who used to be the apple of his wife's eye finds that he must compete for her attention amid a throng of children she seems to love much more than she loves him—and then, as parenthood changes and gentles him, he learns that competition with one's kids is kind of depressing, so he accepts the new shape of his love life.

Things that have helped me include speaking up to say that I feel like I'm not being listened to (this was unpleasant, and I wish I'd figured out a calm way to do it rather than yowling out of anger and hurt, but because the person I yowled at responded with understanding, it did help); figuring out which methods of communication work best for me (i.e., email is less stressful than phone); praying for humility in my friendships; and using the standard couples' trick of intentionally recalling the many times my friends have stood by me. It's a cliché, but it's true, that we find it easy to remember all the support we've given others but hard to remember how much we've needed and received ourselves. Making a conscious effort to remember and be grateful for everything my friends have done for me has carried me through a lot of frustration.

And it's helpful to try to see things from the other person's perspective. I remember there was one day when I was intensely frustrated with a close friend because she wasn't doing something that I perceived as easy and simple, which would obviously vastly improve her life. Why was she procrastinating? Why was she making things so *hard?*

"This," I suddenly realized, "is probably a little bit like how she felt when I was still drinking."

Like marriages, good friendships take work. Like marriages, they get better with age, and if you can stick it out through the tough times, they will sustain you later.

Some of the best writing on Christian faith and loneliness I've found is in Wesley Hill's book *Washed and Waiting.* I've focused on *overcoming* loneliness, but that probably isn't the best way to understand it as a Christian. Hill focuses on loneliness as a way to see God working in our lives. He quotes the fourteenth-century Persian poet Hafiz:

> Don't
> Surrender
> Your loneliness so quickly.
> Let it cut more
> Deep.
>
> Let it ferment and season you
> As few human
> Or even divine ingredients can.[7]

Hill's book expresses more eloquently than I can what it looks like to trust God through loneliness and through loneliness's frequent companions, such as shame and humiliating awareness of our own neediness. It's important to reach out, to cultivate friendships with those around us; but it is even more important to remember that loneliness may be one way God is drawing us closer to him. When we feel most exposed, that's when we are being sheltered in Christ's wounds.

Or as Hill wrote, quoting Fr. Henri Nouwen, "The wound of loneliness is like the Grand Canyon, Nouwen wrote, 'a deep incision on the surface of our existence which has become an inexhaustible source of beauty and self-understanding.'"[8]

conclusion

The Two Crowns

After all this angst and drama, did the exiled soldier finally find her home in the Catholic Church?

Well . . . sort of. On one of the days I played with the little plastic soldier, I probably watched the 1982 animated classic *The Last Unicorn* because I was tender-headed and I wouldn't let my mom brush my hair unless I was watching my favorite movie. (These hours will be counted against her time in purgatory, I do not doubt.) And one of the great lines from that wise, funny movie comes when the shlimazl of a magician, Schmendrick, points out to the unicorn, "There are no happy endings—because nothing ends."

So too in the spiritual life. Many things are better for me now than they were when I was a child or when I was a new convert. My relationship with God is much deeper, I think, and I hope it will get deeper still. But I'm not "at home" in the Catholic Church, and I doubt I ever will be—at least not in this life. There's a place for grateful praise of the Church, of her beauty and her history and the flaming faith of her saints. There's also a place for ambivalence, wry resignation, skepticism of popes and prelates (put not your trust in princes of the Church), and hanging on in spite of the Church as we perceive her.

I hope there's room in the worldview I've sketched out here for that grim, gallows-humor faith, which is sometimes the only kind of faith we have and sometimes—sometimes, sometimes— the kind of faith our lives require. Sometimes it's the only thing that answers the situation.

It's hard to capture in one book all of the moods and seasons of Christian faith. From the very beginning, scripture tells us, the story of the faithful is also the story of doubt, temptation, suffering (both earned and gratuitous), resistance to the truth, humiliation, and despair. In the Rosary both the joyful and sorrowful elements of the lives of Jesus and Mary find their resolution in the final set of Glorious Mysteries, which reveal the meaning of their previous joy and suffering but don't simply erase those emotions and experiences.

I find that writing on gay Catholic life—including my own—has a tendency to overemphasize one mood of faith. I tend to be too sunny-side-up, focusing on the possibility of sublimation and on the love and joy we can find by following our vocations. Other writers tend toward the gloomy side of the path, viewing celibate gay life as mostly a cross and a vale of tears.

In this book I've tried to suggest that if you are gay / same-sex attracted, and you attempt fidelity to the Church's teaching on chastity, your life will be like other Christians' lives—even though it is more misunderstood and marginalized than many of those lives. You do have a vocation, probably more than one. Each of those vocations will come with Jesus' crown of thorns and Mary's crown of stars.

Both the joy and the suffering are real. In this book, I've tried to do two obvious things: reduce the unnecessary suffering and indicate possible paths toward joy. But nobody is happy and at peace with herself all the time. The third task of the book, which has surfaced here and there but has been a much quieter theme, is suggesting that our suffering does have meaning and can be offered to God. It can unite us with Christ's own suffering and conform us more fully to him. We can't always see this while we're in pain; a lot of the time, you do have to just put your head down and endure. But there will be times when you can begin to understand your suffering and see it as part of your relationship with God.

   Both crowns are real. Both the crown of thorns and the crown of stars will be a part of your own life—and you are called to them both by the God who loves you.

Acknowledgments

Very few worthwhile things are created alone. This book required the attention and support of a large group of people. I'm deeply grateful to everyone who read the manuscript during its development, including Calah Alexander, Maggie Gallagher, Pascal-Emmanuel Gobry, Joshua Gonnerman, Wesley Hill, Helen Rittelmeyer, Melinda Selmys, and Nicola Wilson; and my editors, Kristi McDonald and Robert Hamma, who saved me from several embarrassing errors. Obviously all remaining errors of fact, judgment, and taste are mine alone.

I've benefited immensely from others' thinking on these subjects, including the authors and commenters at the blog Spiritual Friendship. I wrote the first draft while I was living with my parents, who put up with me graciously and did not ask when I was planning to get a real job. Emmy Chang, Fr. Kevin Regan, and Fr. Paul Dressler kept me from being more flamboyantly disastrous than usual. And perhaps some praise should go to Charles Alan Garland, who lived in a very different time. "When you don't know what to do, throw a party."

appendix one

Further Resources

There are a surprising number of resources out there for LGBT /
same-sex attracted Catholics and other Christians. None of them
is perfect. I've tried to indicate the ones that have helped me most,
but maybe the most important thing to say at the outset of this
section is that everyone's needs are different, and the resources
that work best for one person may leave another person angry,
alienated, or simply bored. I think because chaste gay / same-sex
attracted life is so unrepresented in mainstream media, there's a
tendency to seize on one good-enough (or even not good-enough)
resource and say, "You should just do X!" or, "Have you heard of
X? They're the best." Straight people do this (I'm amazed at how
many straight people who have never in their lives attended a
Courage or Encourage meeting are nonetheless convinced that it
is a universal solution to the problem of Catholic homosexuals)
but honestly, we do it too, pushing on others the resources which
have worked for us.

Official Statements of the Catholic Church

These may be the most obvious places to start—though not perhaps the most helpful. The *Catechism* is not the fullness of the
faith, and if you want to know how God is calling you then you
should look to the lives of the saints rather than the position
statements of the bishops' conferences. Still, let's take a look at the
Catechism, since many people are unaware of its full description
of the Catholic position on homosexuality. You can find these
passages in paragraphs 2357–2359.

2357 Homosexuality refers to relations between men or between women who experience an exclusive or predominant sexual attraction toward persons of the same sex. It has taken a great variety of forms through the centuries and in different cultures. Its psychological genesis remains largely unexplained. Basing itself on Sacred Scripture, which presents homosexual acts as acts of grave depravity, tradition has always declared that "homosexual acts are intrinsically disordered." They are contrary to the natural law. They close the sexual act to the gift of life. They do not proceed from a genuine affective and sexual complementarity. Under no circumstances can they be approved. (2333)

2358 The number of men and women who have deep-seated homosexual tendencies is not negligible. This inclination, which is objectively disordered, constitutes for most of them a trial. They must be accepted with respect, compassion, and sensitivity. Every sign of unjust discrimination in their regard should be avoided. These persons are called to fulfill God's will in their lives and, if they are Christians, to unite to the sacrifice of the Lord's Cross the difficulties they may encounter from their condition.

2359 Homosexual persons are called to chastity. By the virtues of self-mastery that teach them inner freedom, at times by the support of disinterested friendship, by prayer and sacramental grace, they can and should gradually and resolutely approach Christian perfection. (2347)

The first reference, 2333, refers back to the importance of "the complementarity, needs, and mutual support between the sexes," and the second reference, 2347, leads to this lovely bit about friendship:

> The virtue of chastity blossoms in friendship. It shows the disciple how to follow and imitate him who has chosen us as his friends, who has given himself totally to us and allows us to

participate in his divine estate. Chastity is a promise of immor-
tality. (374)
　　Chastity is expressed notably in friendship with one's
neighbor. Whether it develops between persons of the same
or opposite sex, friendship represents a great good for all. It
leads to spiritual communion.

Note the *Catechism's* refreshing agnosticism about, and lack of
focus on, the origin of homosexuality. And note the prohibition
on "[e]very sign of unjust discrimination." You may argue that
the real controversies are all about *which* forms of discrimination are unjust. That's fair, but the vagueness of the *Catechism's*
language is in my opinion a feature rather than a bug, since it's
trying to communicate a universal truth to Catholics in a startling
variety of political systems and social contexts. You may also—
and here I'd agree with you completely—note how poorly the
Church's official representatives, including the Catholic school
system, often do at living up to this task of avoiding unjust discrimination. These failures of love are occasions for prayerful
activism rather than prayerful acceptance.

　　In 1986 then-Cardinal Joseph Ratzinger issued a "Letter to the
Bishops of the Catholic Church on the Pastoral Care of Homosexual Persons."[1] This statement is not a jewel in the Church's
crown, I'm sorry to say.

　　The letter includes biblical exegesis that is probably too curt
to be responsible: The statement that St. Paul "lists those who
behave in a homosexual fashion among those who shall not enter
the Kingdom of God" does not actually mean that the Catholic Church teaches that everybody who has gay sex will go to
hell. The letter uses AIDS as a cudgel to try to scare gay people straight, and implies that gay liberation provoked anti-gay
violence.

It includes certain official formulations that I find especially unilluminating:

> In the discussion which followed the publication of the Declaration, however, an overly benign interpretation was given to the homosexual condition itself, some going so far as to call it neutral, or even good. Although the particular inclination of the homosexual person is not a sin, it is a more or less strong tendency ordered toward an intrinsic moral evil; and thus the inclination itself must be seen as an objective disorder.
>
> Therefore special concern and pastoral attention should be directed toward those who have this condition, lest they be led to believe that the living out of this orientation in homosexual activity is a morally acceptable option. It is not.

This passage encapsulates my basic problem with the jargon of "objective disorder" when applied to homosexuality. It assumes a clear distinction between sexual desire and other forms of love, when I think the more vague term "same-sex attraction" does more justice to the complexity of our desires. If I make soup for my girlfriend, I'm "acting on my lesbian desires" insofar as I'm motivated by our relationship, which is a lesbian one; and yet these actions are obviously not prohibited by the catechism. To call homosexuality "objectively disordered," always directed toward and fulfilled in sexual acts, is to reduce the tangle of emotional experiences we've decided to call "homosexuality" to only those expressions that are forbidden by the *Catechism* and ignore all the expressions that aren't.

I view "objectively disordered" as theological jargon that attempts to express something true but will be refined and perhaps even rejected as time goes by. The teaching will not change, but the jargon with which the teaching is articulated obviously does change and will change again. Some readers of this book may be a part of that change; I certainly hope so.

Anyway, for the purposes of this appendix it's probably enough to note that you can object to some of the ways the bishops, the theologians, and even the pope talk about homosexuality without dissenting from the teachings of the Church.

Beyond this well-known Vatican intervention, there have been statements by a few national bishops' conferences. The US Conference of Catholic Bishops in 1997 issued the statement "Always Our Children,"[2] which is addressed primarily to the parents of gay Catholics. It is mostly quite good, and if your parents are struggling with accepting your sexuality and a bishops' statement would help them, you might suggest that they read it. It will both reassure and challenge them: "Your child may need you and the family now more than ever. He or she is still the same person. This child, who has always been God's gift to you, may now be the cause of another gift: your family becoming more honest, respectful, and supportive. Yes, your love can be tested by this reality, but it can also grow stronger through your struggle to respond lovingly."

This is an area where the Church hierarchy's level of understanding and its ability to convey the truth clearly and humbly are changing fast. Future statements will likely be better than these.

Books

Here is a list of all the books I have read on gay Christian or gay Christian–adjacent life that I or my friends have found helpful. I've starred the ones I especially and personally recommend.

* Bray, Alan, *The Friend* (Chicago, IL: University of Chicago Press, 2003).
If you've read this far, you already know why I want you to read this book.

Cameli, Louis J., *Catholic Teaching on Homosexuality: New Paths to Understanding* (Notre Dame, IN: Ave Maria Press, 2012).
A sensitive and imaginative reframing of Catholic teaching; too theoretical and abstract for my own tastes.

Groeschel, Benedict, *The Courage to Be Chaste* (Mahwah, NJ: Paulist Press, 1985).
General guidance on chastity that grew out of a request for Groeschel to write something for the members of Courage.

* Hill, Wesley, *Washed and Waiting: Reflections on Christian Faithfulness and Homosexuality* (Grand Rapids, MI: Zondervan, 2010).
In my opinion, the best book we have so far.

Hopko, Thomas, *Christian Faith and Same-Sex Attraction: Eastern Orthodox Reflections* (Ben Lomond, CA: Conciliar Press, 2006).
Mostly a re-presentation of the basic Orthodox teachings on sin, grace, and obedience; the material specifically on homosexuality is the weakest.

Morrison, David, *Beyond Gay* (Huntington, IN: Our Sunday Visitor Publishing Division, 1999).
A personal story of accepting Christian chastity while in a loving gay partnership.

Paris, Jenell Williams, *The End of Sexual Identity: Why Sex Is Too Important to Define Who We Are* (Downers Grove, IL: InterVarsity Press, 2011).
An attempt to deconstruct sexual identity categories for Christians.

Pearce, Joseph, *The Unmasking of Oscar Wilde* (San Francisco, CA: Ignatius Press, 2004).
A somewhat pushy reading of Wilde as Catholic; I liked it, and it's a good counterpoint to the also-fascinating *Decadence and Catholicism* by Ellis Hanson (Cambridge, MA: Harvard University Press, 1997).

* Roberts, Christopher Chenault, *Creation and Covenant: The Significance of Sexual Difference in the Moral Theology of Marriage* (New York, NY: T & T Clark International, 2007).
A sensitive, readable theological defense of the traditional Christian teaching on marriage and critique of Christian arguments for gay marriage.

* Roden, Frederick S., *Same-Sex Desire in Victorian Religious Culture* (New York, NY: Palgrave Macmillan, 2002).
Highly recommended for those who can stomach queer theory; passionate and countercultural look at the appeal of Catholicism and Anglo-Catholicism for same-sex attracted Victorians, mostly artists and priests.

Selmys, Melinda, *Sexual Authenticity: An Intimate Reflection on Homosexuality and Catholicism* (Huntington, IN: Our Sunday Visitor Publishing Division, 2009).
A very personal book by a lesbian who fell in love with a man and is now married with children.

* Selmys, Melinda, *Sexual Authenticity: More Reflections* (CreateSpace, 2014).
A fascinating and lovable exploration of how Selmys' thinking on LGBTQ issues has changed over the years.

Blogs

These days some of the best writing and thinking on the intersection of homosexuality and Christianity can be found online.

While there is no substitute for in-real-life friendship, blogs are a good place to find others who are wrestling with these issues. I've been thrilled to see how many gay Christian bloggers have come out just in the past few months; by the time you read this book, there will be many more. You might start with *Spiritual Friendship*, http://spiritualfriendship.org. Started by Ron Belgau, this blog brings together many different voices, mostly but not exclusively the voices of celibate gay Christians. Wesley Hill, Melinda Selmys, and I are contributors.

Browse the blogroll there and you'll find many more people, from a wide variety of backgrounds. There is no reason to feel as unique or as isolated as I did when I converted.

Courage

Courage and Encourage are the officially approved Catholic ministries to people with same-sex attraction (Courage) and their loved ones (Encourage). The major benefit of Courage, in my opinion, is simply that it lets you meet other people who may be dealing with somewhat similar issues. It will also connect you to a priest, so if you are concerned with finding a confessor who is experienced at speaking with people with same-sex attraction, this may be a good place to look.

Problems I've heard about from participants (I don't know of any research data on these questions) include a heavy preponderance of men and dearth of women and a willingness to promote chintzy psychological theorists. I would also suggest that the adaptation of AA's Twelve Steps to promote chastity rather than sobriety means that the group may be most relevant for people who are troubled by sexual "acting out" and feel that their sexual urges are, in the AA term, "unmanageable."

I have several friends who have been involved with Courage to one extent or another, but it's worth noting that *all* of them eventually scaled back their involvement, partly due to increasing spiritual maturity but partly due to increasing differences with the group's philosophy and practice. If you find that Courage supports you in your chastity and your overall vocation, it's a good fit for you. If you don't, though, you're under no obligation to go there. Friendships, online support, and/or spiritual direction can help you immensely in either case.

Spiritual Direction

"Spiritual direction" is Catholic jargon for finding a priest or layperson you can meet with regularly to get guidance in strengthening your relationship with God. It's a very individual process: I was up-front about the fact that I didn't expect much actual "direction" and primarily wanted a confessor to whom I could be accountable and open about my drinking problem. Other people may want more specific instructions, more focus on the structure of their prayer life, or more emphasis on discerning and pursuing their vocation. Spiritual direction is basically a way of getting an outside opinion on your spiritual life—and not just any outside opinion, but the opinion of someone who has, typically, seen a lot of other Christians working on their various issues. This experience, ideally, gives your director a sense of how individual our struggles and vocations can be—one size definitely doesn't fit all—but also a repertoire of practices and interventions that have been helpful to others and may help you as well.

Spiritual directors come from a variety of different traditions within the Catholic faith and often have different theories about how spiritual direction should work—how much advice should be given versus how much the one being given advice should figure things out for herself, for example. So it's worth asking questions up front and "shopping around" if your first experience seems pointless or damaging. You don't need to mistrust your instincts so thoroughly that you simply accept the first person who's willing to work with you.

If you work with a priest, he may also be your regular confessor, though you can still go to confession with someone else whenever you want to. In spiritual direction, as in therapy, you need to find someone who is willing to work with you where you are, rather than imposing his own beliefs and "system" on you. If you feel like your spiritual director isn't listening or consistently pushes a narrative of your life that feels alien, especially if that narrative seems unhelpfully concerned with explaining the origins of your sexual orientation, it is always OK to seek another spiritual director. It may be worth your while to mention your sexual orientation and your chastity in the first meeting, even if it isn't the main reason you're there, if you're not sure how your spiritual director will respond.

In Orthodox churches, the parish priest often acts as a "spiritual father" for those seeking guidance. He would also be your regular confessor. Orthodox can also seek out spiritual guidance outside the parish—for example, at a local monastery.

Protestant churches may or may not have somewhat parallel institutions. Many Protestants have started asking friends of theirs to fulfill somewhat similar roles in their lives, often reciprocally, as the friends serve as "accountability partners" for each other. This has all the benefits and drawbacks you would expect from mixing friendship and spiritual leadership. It may be best to ask your pastor or a mentor what (and whom) he or she would recommend.

appendix two
Frequently Asked Questions

Advice from strangers is Russian roulette. Most of your personal and family dilemmas can only be addressed by people with deep knowledge of and love for everyone involved. But I do get some recurring questions, and I'll try to say something useful here about how to approach these questions. The first two sections address questions I get from straight people, and the rest address questions from gay / same-sex attracted people.

How do I talk to my gay friends and family?

This is by far the most common thing straight people ask me.

The answer may depend on your family's "style": Some families are full of happy warriors, who think the dinner table is the *best* place to discuss politics and religion. But many people feel like their gay friends or relatives are uniquely sensitive about questions of religion and homosexuality. If you are unsure how they'd react to your opening a conversation about what Jesus thinks of the gays, I would strongly suggest *not opening that conversation*. Christians guilt-trip ourselves into being awful toward our friends because we think we need to be "witnesses to the Gospel." I've done that. It ends up becoming "harassment for Jesus." Consider taking a leaf from the AA handbook and focusing on "attraction, not promotion": Don't push God.

I tend to think that conversations about Christianity in general, and its understanding of homosexuality in particular, go best when the non-Christian asks the questions rather than being told what to care about.

Should I go to my friend's/sister's/someone's gay wedding? In general, how should I treat my friends' or relatives' partners? How can I teach my children the Catholic viewpoint without rejecting those who live an active gay lifestyle?

My sense is that straight Catholic parents are very aware of the ways that the surrounding culture militates against their attempts to teach their children sexual morality. They may be less focused on the ways our culture militates against the attempt to teach children about mercy, hospitality, and unconditional love. We live in an individualistic culture where obligations to others, especially obligations that weren't chosen, are often subordinated to personal wants. And children, in my experience, have a hard time understanding or accepting unconditional love. They'll often assume that your love is conditional on good behavior unless they *see* otherwise. So keeping strong, close ties with family members who have left the Church or who are not practicing their faith can be a *good* lesson for kids, albeit a complicated one.

On the one hand, in the Gospel of Luke Jesus tells us, "If any man come to me, and hate not his father, and mother, and wife, and children, and brethren, and sisters, yea, and his own life also, he cannot be my disciple" (Lk 14:26). Our families can't become reasons to reject God or the Church. But rejecting the bonds of love should be a sacrifice like the sacrifice of one's own life—a last resort. Moreover, morality doesn't start and end with sexual morality. Welcoming and cherishing one's family with humility and patience is also a major part of Christian morality. Don't put the need to protect and educate your children above the need to see and welcome Christ in the form of your gay, partnered sibling.

So I would suggest finding what is good in your sibling's gay marriage or partnership. (This is assuming that you would *not* be equally concerned about the relationship if it were a heterosexual marriage. Obviously if your sister or brother is in an abusive gay relationship, the issues are very different.) Remember that this person and this love may actually be a part of your sibling's vocation. God may be calling him or her to love this specific partner, even though that love shouldn't be expressed sexually. Ask yourself which actions will be most likely to help your sibling or friend to see your faith as a source of humility, generosity, and tenderness, rather than convincing him or her that Christianity makes even good people bad. You want the people around you to feel safe in coming to you when and if they do have questions about faith. If you've come across as rejecting them in the name of religion or considering their relationships fake, it isn't very likely that they will want to hear more about your God.

I went to an ex-gay conference many years ago where Joe Dallas suggested that parents of gay teens ask themselves, "What is God trying to change in *me* through this relationship?" While I didn't agree with all of Dallas's presentation, this line struck me as a thoughtful way to approach any difficult family situation.

If your friends or family members insist that simply upholding the Catholic beliefs on marriage and sexuality make you hateful or bigoted, that isn't something you can or should compromise on, and they shouldn't ask you to compromise your faith. But if they're simply asking you not to bring up sexual morality at Thanksgiving when they say their partner is coming to dinner, then I'd just thank them for the sweet potatoes.

On the specific subject of attending gay weddings, well, I've been to one, so that's my position. Here are some things to consider: If you don't attend, will you be cutting yourself off from future contact with friends or family? You can't witness to people you never speak to anymore. Would you attend the opposite-sex wedding of a Catholic who had previously been validly married in the Church but divorced? If so, it's worth asking whether this situation is so different. Does your sibling or friend know that you're an orthodox Catholic? If so, I doubt he or she will assume that you suddenly changed your mind. If not, or if you're unsure what he or she thinks you believe, would it be possible to sit down and talk it out? This will depend *a lot* on your relationship with the person and on both parties' styles of interaction. But you *may* be able to say something like, "Look, by inviting me to attend this ceremony you're asking me to support your relationship. I do support the love and care you show each other, and I always will—that's something I'm prepared to promise. I don't support the sexual side of your relationship; it's a matter of my faith, and it isn't something I am likely to change my mind on. But if support for your love is 'enough,' I'm there." This may open a conversation you two should have had already. But it's a painfully delicate conversation, happening at a time when your interlocutor is under a ton of stress—preparing for a wedding isn't the greatest time for heart-to-heart family talks or intense religious debates. So be aware that it might not be a good idea to even have this conversation at this time, if it might blow up into a fight. I would err on the side of showing support.

In general, people are much more likely to understand and accept your claim that you support them as people, even if you don't support everything they do, if they can *see* the "support" part. Humans tend to exaggerate negatives and forget about positives. So the more real, unarguable support you can give, the better.

I also think of Meredith's decision to attend my Baptism, which I mentioned in chapter 3. I was under no illusions that she suddenly agreed with my decision to enter the Church. In a way, her disagreement with my decision made her attendance all the more moving—it was purely an act of friendship, an act of welcome and love for me as a person.

And finally, it may help to keep in mind that the conflict may reappear in a mirror image from their perspective. They may be having a hard time figuring out how to teach their own children to respect Uncle Joe and Aunt Mary even though they have major, emotionally fraught differences with some of Joe and Mary's beliefs. All of us have a chance to be a good example for others—or a cautionary tale. Which will you be to the gay, non-celibate people who love you?

Should I come out?

Obviously, there are degrees of being "out": We often tell our friends before our family, for example. I don't think you necessarily have a responsibility to come out, especially if doing so would cause severe consequences for your family life.

I will say, though, that life in the closet brings many temptations to sin. You're tempted to hold your friends at arm's length. You're pushed into situations where you may end up blurting out a lie because you aren't prepared to admit the truth. You may find yourself tempted to denigrate other gay people, laugh along with homophobic jokes, or focus attention on someone else's homosexuality to distract attention from your own.

Being closeted also may deprive you of the experience of having someone accept who you *are*, not who you appear to be. Many gay/same-sex attracted people have a small, destructive voice that whispers, "They won't love you once they find out." Proving that voice wrong can be an extraordinarily powerful moment of healing. And if you come out to enough people, it *will* be proved wrong, since even if you're rejected by some people you deeply care about, you'll be accepted and reassured by many others. Coming out often allows us to believe in God's own promises of love in a way we couldn't before.

The opportunity you miss to be loved for who you are, if you stay closeted, is also missed by those around you. They lose the opportunity to show you that they do love and accept you. You may not be giving them enough credit.

Finally, you miss the opportunity to be a witness to chastity and fidelity—although that "opportunity" comes with a lot of pressure to be perfect, which may be one reason to use caution as you come out, especially if you have perfectionist tendencies already. Be sure that you have some friends you can be real with about your ongoing struggles or sins, whether they're obviously related to sexuality or not, so that you don't feel like you have to be a perfect poster gay.

I think the loneliness and isolation of the closet are usually the biggest sources of pain, but the underestimation of those around you is also draining—you may spend a lot of time reminding yourself of why it isn't a good idea to come out, which means reminding yourself of your own negative judgments of the people around you and their ability to accept you.

Your own situation may not permit you to come out right now, and you may decide that it simply isn't right for you: because your sexuality is complicated; because you're now married and you don't want your spouse to face judgments and criticism; because you never had a particularly strong connection to gay communities and your same-sex attraction isn't a big day-to-day concern for you; because you don't want to lock yourself in to one identity at an early age (although really, it's OK to say you were wrong, or that you used to be more bisexual than you are now); or any other reason. But in every case I can think of among my friends, coming out was overall a positive experience for them. For some it brought family conflict; for others it led to familial acceptance and reconciliation. For *everyone*, though, it deepened friendships and let them be vulnerable and receive support in an area where for years they had been isolated.

Should I seek therapy to heal my homosexuality?

Two kinds of people ask this question: People who really want to stop being gay, and people who really don't want that—but wonder if they should. For people in the second camp I would say, *Pray*. Pray for acceptance of whatever God chooses to do with this part of your life. Pray so that you can accept it if he heals you in ways you didn't particularly want to be healed. If this question continues to concern you, consider seeking spiritual direction with someone who understands that "reparative therapy" is often based on dubious psychological theories and assumptions. This person should be someone who won't pressure you to stop identifying as gay or seek specific kinds of therapy.

For people in the first camp I would say, *Research*. I mean, you should pray too! But research is hugely important here. One great place to start is *Disputed Mutability*, http://disputedmutability. wordpress.com, a blog by a woman who identified as ex-gay for a while and received a lot of help through that approach but also has sharp criticisms of the ex-gay world. You can also look at other blogs and websites by ex-gay and "ex-ex-gay" writers, looking for people who did the kinds of therapy you're most interested in. If you have a specific therapist in mind, look that person up online and read both praise and criticism, if you can find it.

In general, keep in mind that there are three separate categories or layers of therapy here: healing emotional wounds that keep you from leading a full life or living out your vocation; healing emotional wounds specifically related to the formation of your sexuality; and developing a different sexual orientation. So, for example, *even if* a bad relationship with your father contributed to the development of your sexual orientation, you can work on that relationship or its effects on your life without wanting and certainly without experiencing any change in your orientation.

I would argue that the first layer is the most important and the third the least, but even if you disagree with how I rank them, it's worth seeking out a therapist who acknowledges the difference between the layers and accepts your assessment of their ranking.

How do I deal with crushes? In terms of physical affection, how far can you go?

Ah, the classic catechism-class question!

This one is even harder to answer in the abstract than most of these questions. I've seen people turn crushes into friendships; I've seen people make that attempt and get disappointed, with the friendship slowly breaking up under the pressure of one-sided attraction; I've seen people start by trying to turn crushes into friendship and end by leaving the Church and becoming sexually active (often not with the person they had the original crush on).

It may help to keep the various alternative futures in mind from the beginning and stay honest about what they would entail. That might help you remember the necessity of putting your relationship with God *first*. That relationship, like every love relationship, may sometimes strengthen your other loves but it may sometimes come into conflict with them. Like every other love relationship, only more so, it will require sacrifices, and there will be times when you have to say no to yourself or to someone else in order to continue saying yes to God and to your relationship with God.

It may also be helpful to remember that you can't control the outcomes here. If you have a crush on someone, and he rejects your friendship and even gets disturbed by the thought that you were attracted to him, that isn't actually your fault—that's a series of feelings and actions on *his* part.

Ask yourself how your spiritual life is affected. When you're around this person are you kind of rapturously grateful to God for the chance to be with them? Are you able to talk to other people too or do you obsessively focus on this one person? Are you jealous? Are you more charitable than usual (toward everybody) because they make you feel happy and you want to please them? When you're away from this person do you find yourself distracted from prayer by thoughts of them, or do you find yourself less likely to continue your prayer practices—is it harder to motivate yourself to pray and worship? If you go away for a week without them, is there a certain relief and a certain dread at returning to the poignant, suspenseful, exciting state of being near them?

Some of these heady reactions are just part of the emotional roller coaster of a crush. But jealousy, inability to be generous to others, lack of motivation in prayer, and exhausting but addicting drama are all, I think, good signs that you should try taking some serious time away from this person. The harder that sounds, the more useful it might be in clarifying your emotions. See if you can put together a group of people with whom you can continue your preexisting spiritual practices. I don't think this is a great time to add a lot of new practices, but if you find it hard to stay motivated in attending Mass, for example, you can see if any of your (non-crush) friends are free to come with you.

This might be a good concern to bring to spiritual direction.

Of course, if your crush seems to be making you *more* charitable and more fervent in prayer and just generally more thrilled with God, you should think about and prepare for what will happen when the crush fades and even if the friendship itself breaks up. We've all seen "evangelization through eros" among our heterosexual brethren: The new head of Students for Christ is so devout! *And so are his cheekbones!* That initial attraction doesn't mean your renewed faith is necessarily insincere, or merely self-deception masquerading as sublimation. It does mean you shouldn't hang your eternal hopes on this dude's smile.

Some people, myself included, have found it helpful to focus on thanking God for bringing this person into our lives. Specifically, it can be helpful to thank God for her beauty. This allows you to acknowledge that beauty and offer your own heart to the Beauty that created it. It redirects your thoughts toward God and doesn't require you to feel bad for being attracted to someone lovely. There's a lack of judgment there that many people find very spiritually helpful.

This situation is also one reason it's often wise to have several close friends to whom you're open about your sexual orientation—not just one. This is the exact kind of thing you'd want trusted friends' advice on: friends who share or at least respect your religious convictions and who also know what you're like, who can ask questions about what makes you happy these days or point out ways in which your behavior has changed.

In terms of physical affection, I see that as a separate question, although if you're dealing with both at once—a crush with whom you are, or want to be, pretty physically affectionate—you should dial back the handsiness for a while. But most people long for touch even when they're not "in love with" anybody in particular.

Some parts of American culture are more physically affectionate than others, obviously, and unfortunately, men will generally have a much harder time meeting their needs for touch. In 2012, an Arizona high school principal actually used handholding as a punishment for two boys who got in a fight. The boys' photos, showing them holding hands while covering their faces, got posted all over social media, and they were teased and humiliated.[1] In other words, hitting a boy is not shameful but holding his hand is. In a culture where boys holding hands is a humiliating form of punishment, men aren't exactly encouraged to find ways of fulfilling their need for nonsexual forms of physical affection.

Several men have described to me how humiliating it was to have to ask their friends to hug or hold them when they were miserable or just a bit lonely—and yet that was a deeply healing experience for them. This may be an area where you have to go through what Edmund Spenser called "The Gracious Valley of Humiliation" and ask for what you need.

It's also, of course, an area where you need to be honest and aware of your own motivations. But the fact that you *could* deceive yourself by pretending you want to be hugged, when you really want something prohibited by the *Catechism*, isn't actually an argument against hugs. Being physically affectionate with one another is a major way humans give and receive love. It's thoroughly normal to want to hold or be held by people you love.

Actually, of course, what counts as "normal" physical affection varies enormously from culture to culture. A way of interacting with others that reads as bizarrely cold in southern Italy would be totally normal in England (or so period-piece movies have convinced me), and a way of interacting that suggests everyday friendship in one place may come across as overtly sexual in another. If Judas kissed Jesus on the lips today outside a DC coffee shop, my first thought would not be that this was a student greeting his teacher. So one way to think about this question is to ask yourself what you want from physical affection, what *meaning* you want it to have for you, and how you can get that without moving into the realm of gestures you've been raised to consider sexual or tempting.

I've heard that the classic answer to the "How far can you go?" question is, "Use your judgment. But no French kissing." That answer gets at two important truths. First, the "rules," such as they are, exist to serve the virtues of chastity and charity. The point is not to follow the rules but to exercise the virtues. However, man is a rationalizing animal. We're prone to deceiving ourselves and maintaining plausible deniability so that by the time we acknowledge that we're in danger of serious sin, we're already in way over our heads. Most sins aren't spontaneous—we prepare for them by a series of self-comforting, self-indulgent thoughts. If you feel yourself trying to "explain away" your actions, that may be a sign that you're unnecessarily scrupulous, condemning yourself for things that are genuinely innocent. But it may instead mean that you're rationalizing.

Notice that there are two virtues in play here—chastity and charity—and therefore two corresponding vices. The vice that creeps in when we're not practicing chastity is probably obvious. The vice when we're not practicing charity is perhaps less clear and will vary from person to person: a rejection of friendship, a denial of the worth of our own bodies, or a kind of spiritual pride in thinking that we're not so weak that we "need" things like hugs. If we focus solely on protecting our chastity we may more easily fall into these other problems.

What if following the Church's teaching here is terrible for my mental health?

You're probably sick of hearing me say, "It depends," so let me instead suggest that there's a spectrum of responses here, depending on how acute your misery is and what kinds of hope and encouragement you tend to respond to. I'll start at the least-comforting end: sometimes the only response in this situation is, "This is your cross." This is the place where you're being called to imitate the most devastating and awful parts of the life of Christ.

There's a cultural component to your anguish here, if it helps to point that out. We're trained to think that anguish is always a sign that something's wrong: that we're doing something wrong. That's often true but not always. Jesus wasn't doing anything wrong in Gethsemane. Imitation of Christ is the task of all Christians, and many of us are not spared the most painful parts of that imitation.

And you're not called to be the picture of bourgeois mental health. Many of the saints exhibit behavior for which we can find diagnoses in the DSM-V. You don't have to feel ashamed of your misery; it doesn't mean you're being a bad Christian; it doesn't mean that God has forgotten you; and it doesn't mean that you aren't working hard enough or loving God enough. Sometimes it means that you are being held very close to Christ, in his sacred wounds.

That said, there's also a middle point on the spectrum, which is: try bringing other areas of your life more deeply in line with God's will for you. Maybe forget about this area for a little while. Don't torture yourself because you're not doing everything all at once.

If you completely put sexual questions aside, and gave yourself entire freedom to act in that sphere, I'm sure there would still be plenty of other areas where your spiritual life is fairly ragged and catawampus. As you begin to bring those areas to God, humbly and prayerfully, you may find that you are slowly becoming more ready to bring sexual questions to him as well. Your overall trust in God and/or the Church may grow to the point that you no longer view the historical Christian understanding of chastity as a psychic death sentence. But even if that doesn't happen, you will still have done well to abandon yourself to God in these other areas of your life. He knows the pain and pressures you face, and he is thrilled by every movement you make toward him. Nothing you do for love of him is insufficient or pointless.

And then, too, the final point on the spectrum, which for some people will be the overridingly important point: God doesn't want you to kill yourself.

What if I'm already in a long-term, committed partnership, but I am starting to accept (or I'm starting to be troubled by the possibility of accepting) the Christian teaching? What if my same-sex partner and I have gotten married or had a commitment ceremony? What if we're raising children?

This is a very tough situation where I'm hesitant to say too much. I don't think your vows become meaningless if you change your beliefs about the proper role of sexuality in your relationship. You've still vowed, presumably, to love and cherish this person, and those are unequivocally good things. This person may still be a major part of your vocation. Certainly if you're raising kids then the well-being of those children should be your primary concern, and kids really need a home with stability and the secure knowledge that the adults who raise them are working together as a family unit.

There are some gay couples who have made this transition from a sexually active partnership to a chaste one. In 1999 the *Boston Globe* profiled one such couple, Steven Durost and Mike Howatt. At the time the article was written Durost and Howatt had been living celibately for five years, and were deeply involved in ex-gay religious and therapeutic groups. Reading the *Globe* piece gives you a sense of how tough and how humiliatingly hard to explain this road can be. And many people won't want to (and shouldn't) take the specific ex-gay path Durost and Howatt chose. But a gay couple in which at least one partner wants to move toward chastity isn't actually doing something completely unprecedented, crazy, and unimaginable.

This is a situation where everyone involved needs to be aware of how much they don't control. You can't control how your partner reacts if you explain your faith or your struggles with faith. It may be helpful to emphasize that you aren't choosing what you believe. You didn't sit down and pick this faith in order to be difficult or because you no longer love your partner. The idea that we "choose" our religious beliefs—or our ethical beliefs—is much more false than true, and you can see that for yourself if you try to *sincerely* choose to see the world from the point of view of an Orthodox Jew, or a Mormon, or an atheist, whatever it is that you know you're not. Your choice is whether to acknowledge what you believe or deny it. Denying it would mean denying your conscience—the very thing your partner relies upon to keep you loving, faithful, honest, and generous. A good partnership can't be based on one person's denial of conscience.

But this is a very hard situation and one in which both partners will face a lot of judgment from others no matter what they end up doing. If you can possibly find a spiritual director whom *both* of you relate to, and who is able to tell the difference between his personal opinion and the demands of the faith, seeing this director both separately and with your partner may be a helpful step. You may find that you can't move toward chastity as fast as you'd like to or think you should—this is an experience painfully familiar to many heterosexual couples—and you need a confessor (if you're Catholic) who will help you be patient with yourself and your partner. You need people in your life, ideally both your confessor and at least one close friend, who will encourage you rather than either condemning you for not living up to your beliefs immediately *or* taking difficulties with chastity or with your relationship as a sign that you shouldn't attempt Christian sexual morality at all.

It may be helpful to go to Mass or other services with your partner, or anywhere else where he or she can see the beauty, hope, or truth that you find in Christ. The more you can show your partner what the faith *is* to you, in areas unrelated to sexuality, the more he or she may be able to understand why you're willing to change both your own life and theirs so drastically.

But in the end, neither of you need to understand exactly why the other person believes what they do. We love one another without understanding one another all the time.

appendix three

Making the Church a Place of Welcome for Same-Sex Attracted Christians

Here are seven suggestions for cultural change within the Christian churches. These are only one woman's opinion and only a beginning. You may want to modify my ideas or come up with something better. I can't wait to hear from readers about what I missed! But if you're looking for a practical place to start, consider doing one of these things now.

Actually, wait. Before I make my suggestions, let me offer a caution about motives. I think a lot of the time, Christians are tempted to instrumentalize love—to turn our love and service to others into a form of advertising for Jesus. We ask, "How can we convince gay people that we're not their enemies?" or even, "How can we get gay people to listen to us?" instead of, "How can we love the gay people around us, including those who feel most hostile or excluded?"

Mixed motives aren't the worst things in the world. But they do set you up for a lot of disappointment, if you do the hard work of love and don't get the credit you feel you deserve for it. I've spoken to campus ministers who tried to form alliances with campus LGBT groups only to be told that their views and their presence were unwelcome. Some of that rejection may have occurred because we can sometimes tell when people are only being nice in order to soften us up for a pitch. But sometimes the rejection happened just because other people aren't under your control. They aren't going to respond the way you want them to, no matter how gentle and loving you are. Going in with the attitude that you're making sacrifices or doing hard work in order to attain respect or other positive responses from other people sets you up for failure—and resentment.

In the '80s, John Cardinal O'Connor of New York opposed laws that would prohibit employers from discriminating on the basis of sexual orientation, and opposed condom distribution, saying that condoms had a failure rate "as high as fifty percent." He also did something else, though: He turned St. Clare's Hospital into an impromptu AIDS hospice, and on some nights, the cardinal himself would come into the hospital dressed as your basic priest. Introducing himself as "Father John," he would bathe the patients, clean their bedpans, and do whatever other tasks were needed to minister to their bodies and souls. He made himself available to them and vulnerable to them, at a time when AIDS was as stigmatized as biblical leprosy. And what did he win for this? ACT-UP protested inside St. Patrick's Cathedral and desecrated the Host.

They shouldn't have done that. But at the same time, their actions don't make *his* actions a failure. Cardinal O'Connor's treatment of AIDS patients would have been a failure if he conceived it as a public-relations mission to the gay community. If he conceived it, instead, as service to the particular people whose sheets he changed, then the small acts of caring were their own reward.

The reward for loving gay people better isn't better PR, or even more souls saved, although of course I do hope that happens. The reward for loving gay people better is that you love gay people better. And in them you love Christ.

OK, now that I've gotten that off my chest, here are the suggestions.

Come out. This is not something I recommend to everyone regardless of circumstances, as I've said above. However, it's one huge way to change the culture. Right now, very few people even know *of* gay people who try to live chastely—let alone actually knowing any of them personally. That used to be true of gay people in general. The culture changed because people came out. If you let people know that you are gay or same-sex attracted, and you accept the traditional Christian teaching on chastity, that in itself shifts the culture a lot.

It's often uncomfortable and no fun, and you *will* get things wrong. You'll give in to the temptation to be the Voice of a Community. You'll get mad at people who are trying to help you as best they can. You'll get tired and frustrated and sometimes being gay and Christian will seem to take up so much of your time and emotional energy that you almost forget to be a disciple of Christ. (This is not a problem unique to celibate gay people, but a normal problem of witness: the act of witnessing can easily crowd out the One whose witnesses we are.) But if you're able to humbly admit your mistakes and try to extend to others the charity you hope to receive from them, you will do a great, quiet work for God.

Talk about gay issues with a spirit of welcome. This is the equivalent of the previous point for straight people. Brent Bailey, at the blog *Odd Man Out*, wrote:

> As a youth group student and even a freshman in college, I often went weeks or months without hearing Christians mention homosexuality or the gay community, so my ears perked up whenever anyone even vaguely alluded to LGBT issues. Without a doubt, someone's willingness to broach LGBT issues in any sort of positive or empathetic tone is the clearest and most visible indicator they might be prepared to listen to me talk about my sexuality. They may do something as noticeable

as leading a Bible study about homosexuality or as simple as posting a link on Facebook to a story about sexual minorities; but in environments where nontraditional sexuality receives no attention, even the tiniest statement of knowledge or interest can communicate a loud-and-clear message (accurate or not) that this person is the safest person in the room.[1]

Bailey's whole post is worth reading. You don't have to use the exact right lingo or say the perfect thing. Saying *anything* can mean a lot.

Obviously if you're straight, you shouldn't try to speak *for* gay people—you are not the Lorax, and we are not the trees! You'll make mistakes too and get your ego involved, because that's human nature. But if you speak in a way that suggests that you welcome gay and same-sex attracted people, and you don't assume that we all agree about *anything*, people will be more likely to feel that you're someone they can confide in. They're more likely to feel welcome in your group, whatever that group is.

If your church has a moment when you can add a public prayer, you might pray for God to bless gay, lesbian, and/or same-sex attracted people. Or you could pray that all people, regardless of sexual orientation, will find their vocation as they learn to give and receive love. Similarly, a lot of spiritual topics have some aspect that is especially relevant to gay or same-sex attracted people. If you're talking about "guardianship of the tongue," why not include homophobic slurs as something to avoid along with gossip and jokes at other people's expense? If you're talking about how God the Father can offer a model of fatherhood for those whose earthly fathers aren't too loving, why not include the fathers who reject their gay children? There are countless little ways to indicate that you know that gay and same-sex attracted people are part of the Body of Christ.

Get books into libraries! Does your high school, parish, or public library take donations? Why not donate Wesley Hill's book? (Or this one, she said, yanking her light out from under its bushel.) Hill's book is the best for young people, I think, but you could just look at all the books I've praised in Appendix One and choose the one(s) that speak to you. The Internet is great, but nothing can replace a book in a quiet library. A library book won't show up in your search history (especially if you read it there, rather than checking it out), and you can easily run across it without looking for it specifically. That makes library books especially important for the most closeted, scared, or questioning kids.

If the libraries don't want copies, can you talk directly to the guidance counselors and chaplains?

Practice hospitality. If you have kids, ask them what the atmosphere is like in their schools for kids who are gay or perceived to be gay. Let your home be a place of welcome for kids who are having trouble with their own families. Be a refuge.

Support the obligations of friendship in areas you control. Try to minimize the occasions when single people are treated as if they are alone. To take a fairly trivial example, for several years Meredith would come to our family's Thanksgiving, and my sister would include her in the family portrait. If you ask after another person's best friend, welcome her at social events, and understand that sometimes her needs will be uppermost in her friend's mind—all these things can help to strengthen the friendship itself, by offering social support and praise for loving behavior. If you're an employer, can you let employees know that they won't be penalized for taking time off to care for friends in severe need?

Make a family. If it makes sense for you, consider taking a(nother) gay or same-sex attracted Christian into your home.

Can you be brother and sister to someone who needs the shelter of a family home?

That is obviously a huge challenge and not right for everyone. Most people will continue to have families made by blood and marriage, rather than blood and marriage and friendship. But I wonder how many of us have close friends whom we would welcome into our families if we thought to do it or if we had the humility to ask and risk rejection: *You know that you're welcome whenever you want to come here. Here is a key to my place. Have you ever thought about moving in with us, since you're our kids' godfather? This is your Aunt Lisa; she's your mom's best friend.* Again, these options aren't right for everyone. But I think there are many people in our Christian communities—gay or same-sex attracted people, and our married friends—who would do better morally, economically, and spiritually in this way of life. It used to be fairly normal. Many of us grew up with "aunts" and "great-aunts" who were actually the best friend of an aunt or a grandmother. This is a better option than the endless singlehood of "personal watermelons" and chocolate cakes microwaved in coffee mugs.

And last but not least . . .

Be honest about what you're praying for. It's easy to say that we want our churches to be places of refuge and welcome for gay and same-sex attracted people. But then somebody takes us seriously! Somebody shows up with her partner and wants to get their kids baptized, or somebody seeks to become a member of the church and wants to have tough conversations about scripture. Maybe the pastor asks your newly welcome churchgoer to give a testimony of how Jesus rescued him from homosexuality, but he points out that that isn't how he sees his life at all.

Everybody wants to take in a shivering kitten. Not everybody wants to deal with a grown-up cat.

If our churches begin to change to welcome gay and same-sex attracted people, the changes won't stop where the churches might predict they will or want them to. The churches won't be exactly the same as before, only with more people. The churches themselves will change: new concepts of vocation, new questions, new challenges. Things will get weird. If you welcome someone, be ready for them to change you. That's part of what love does to a person.

Notes

Chapter 2: The Botany Club

1.   Dorothy Allison, *Skin: Talking about Sex, Class and Literature* (Ithaca, NY: Firebrand Books, 1994), 77.

2.   The feminist response here is that under patriarchy all women are conditioned to view woman as Other, because we're taught to take the man's viewpoint as normal and the woman's as a deviation from that norm. I agree with that belief to some extent—I've seen countless women respond to the suggestion that they have internalized the "male gaze" with, "Oh my God, is that what that is? That makes so much sense!" and it would be bizarre if patriarchy played no role in how we desire others and how we view ourselves as desiring creatures.

Chapter 3: Evidence for the Prosecution

1.   "[T]here's a special/providence in the fall of a sparrow." William Shakespeare, *Hamlet*. Act V. sc II. (Philadelphia, PA: J.B. Lippincott, 1877), 439.

2.   G. K. Chesterton, *Collected Works of G.K. Chesterton*, vol. 2 (San Francisco, CA: Ignatius Press, 1987), 31.

3.   Thomas Hopko, *Christian Faith and Same-Sex Attraction: Eastern Orthodox Reflections* (Ben Lomond, CA: Conciliar Press, 2006), 66. I don't recommend the book overall (see Appendix One), but I liked this passage.

4.   Catholic.net, "What Child Is This?" http://catholic.net/index.php?option=dedestaca&id=1025 (accessed February 1, 2014).

Chapter 4: Lather, Rinse, Repeat

1.   Robert Andrews, *The Columbia Dictionary of Quotations* (New York, NY: Columbia University Press, 1993), 435.

2.   Nirvana, "Pennyroyal Tea," by Kurt Cobain, on *In Utero*, released in 1993, DGC Records, compact disc.

3.   Alcoholics Anonymous, "The Twelve Steps of Alcoholics Anonymous," http://www.aa.org/lang/en/en_pdfs/smf-121_en.pdf (accessed February 1, 2014).

4.   See, for example, Mark E. Pietrzyk, "Queer Science," *The New Republic* (October 3, 1994): 10–1.

Chapter 5: Three Kinds of Diversity in Gay Christian Lives

1.   As remembered by the author.

2. *Disputed Mutability*, "My Misadventures with 'Healing' Approaches to Homosexuality," http://disputedmutability.wordpress.com/2006/08/03/my-misadventures-with-healing-approaches-to-homosexuality (accessed July 15, 2013).

3. Joseph Volpicelli and Maia Szalavitz, *Recovery Options: The Complete Guide* (New York, NY: John Wiley & Sons, 2000), 151–2.

4. Small Church Music, "Father We Thank Thee Who Hast Planted," http://www.smallchurchmusic3.com/Lyrics/D02/S02270.php (accessed February 1, 2014).

Chapter 6: What Vocation Is and Is Not

1. As remembered by the author.

2. Before I started counseling, I'd heard a lot of bad things about pregnancy centers: that they lied to women and emotionally abused or manipulated them into keeping their babies, for example. I don't doubt that some counselors do lie to or shame women, though I hope those days are mostly behind us. There will always be people who use their position of power over a vulnerable woman to shame her "for her own good," and unfortunately, some of those people have worked at pregnancy centers. In our training, my center always emphasized the need to tell the truth and respect the client, no matter what choice she made. One of the women who led the volunteer training at my own center had been deeply harmed by the way she was treated at a pregnancy center in the '80s. She'd been shamed and made to feel awful about herself, and—this won't surprise anyone who has been in a similar situation—these terrible feelings pushed her toward the abortion she'd been considering, rather than away from it. After her abortion, it took her a long time to come to terms with what had happened to her and the choices she'd made as a result. She trained us so that we would respond with empathy and Christian love, so that none of our clients would experience the cruelty that was inflicted on her.

3. And why does nobody seem to remember that "giving scandal" actually means tempting others, or leading people to think that what is evil is really good—not simply "making good Catholic types uncomfortable or troubled about the state of your soul"? See, for example, paragraphs 2284–2287 of the *Catechism*.

4. C. S. Lewis, *The Screwtape Letters* (San Francisco, CA: HarperOne, 2009), chapter XXVI.

Chapter 7: Friendship in Theology and History

1. Alan Bray, *The Friend* (London, UK: University of Chicago Press, 2003), 25.

2. Ibid., 77.

3. Ibid., 104.

4. Ibid., 116.

5. Ibid., 112 4.

6. Ibid., 316.

7. Ibid., 19.

8. Ibid., 88.

9. Ibid.

10. Ibid., 86–7.

11. Robin Darling Young, "Gay Marriage: Reimagining Church History," *First Things*, November 1994, 43–8.

12. Douglass Roby, "Introduction," *Spiritual Friendship* (Kalamazoo, MI: Cistercian Publications, 1977), 13.

13. Quoted in Roby, 14.

14. Ibid.

15. Aelred of Rievaulx, *Spiritual Friendship* (Kalamazoo: Cistercian Publications, 1977), 115–7.

16. Ibid., 117.

17. Ibid., 78.

18. Ibid., 141.

19. Ibid., 72.

20. Ibid., 92–3.

21. Ibid., 76.

Chapter 8: Spiritual Friendship Today and Tomorrow

1. Some studies even suggest that friendship may be *more* protective of health than familial relationships. See Ethan J. Leib, *Friend v. Friend: The Transformation of Friendship—And What the Law Has to Do with It* (Oxford, UK: Oxford University Press, 2010), 38–9.

2. Alan Chambers, "The New Homosexuality," *Charisma Magazine*, March 10, 2009. http://www.charismamag.com/life/culture/3971-the-new-homosexuality. Chambers has changed many of his views concerning Christian approaches to homosexuality, so I do not intend to imply that he still holds these beliefs today, but his article expresses views which are fairly common in "conservative Christian" circles.

3. Bray, 176.

4. Jonathan Shay, *Achilles in Vietnam: Combat Trauma and the Undoing of Character* (New York, NY: Simon and Schuster, 1995), 41.

5. Hilary Howard, "A Confederacy of Bachelors," *New York Times*, August 3, 2012, http://www.nytimes.com/2012/08/05/nyregion/four-men-sharing-rent-and-friendship-for-18-years.html?_r=1&hpw&pagewanted=all.

6. Karen Walker, "'Always There for Me': Friendship Patterns and Expectations Among Middle- and Working-Class Men and Women," *Sociological Forum* 10, no. 2 (1995): 273–296.

7. See, for example, pp 159–160 of Leib.

8. Cicero, *Laelius on Friendship*, trans. W. A. Falconer, Loeb Classical Library, vol. XX (Boston, MA: Harvard University Press, 1923), xxxiii.86.

9. Bray, 10.

10. For one early lesbian-feminist analysis, see Lillian Faderman, *Surpassing the Love of Men: Romantic Friendship and Love Between Women from the Renaissance to the Present* (New York, NY: William Morrow, 1981), 190–230.

Chapter 9: From Friends to Family

1. Aelred, 99.

2. Amanda Shubert, "Dan Barden," Full Stop, May 14, 2012. http://www.full-stop.net/2012/05/14/interviews/amanda/dan-barden/.

3. Wesley Hill, "Celibacy and Friendship 'After 30,'" *First Things*, December 31, 2012. http://www.firstthings.com/blogs/firstthoughts/2012/12/celibacy-and-friendship-after-30/.

4. Matthew Franklin Jones, "Hospitality," *Gay Subtlety*, August 9, 2012. http://gaysubtlety.wordpress.com/2012/08/09/hospitality/.

Chapter 10: The Church as Home

1. Written by St. Jane Frances de Chantal.

2. http://www.communityofcommunities.info/.

3. Gregg Webb, "Coming Out . . . Orthodox," *Holy Protection*, August 4, 2012. http://holyprotection.wordpress.com/2012/08/04/coming-out-orthodox/.

Chapter 11: Service and Solidarity

1. Dorothy Allison, "Talking to Straight People," *Skin: Talking about Sex, Class and Literature* (Ithaca, NY: Firebrand Books, 1994), 149.

Chapter 12: Challenges Within Your Vocation

1. Matthew Vines, "The Gay Debate: The Bible and Homosexuality," March 10, 2012. http://www.youtube.com/watch?v=ezQjNJUSraY (accessed July 18, 2013).

2.   Brent Bailey, "Family," *Odd Man Out*, January 7, 2013. http://oddman out.net/post/39927898840/family [emphasis added].

3.   She adds, "And may we all, IF POSSIBLE, put down the opium BEFORE we get martyred." But I wanted to focus on the part before that. Heather King, "An Opium-Addicted Saint!" *Shirt of Flame*, November 27, 2011. http:// shirtofflame.blogspot.com/2011/11/opium-addicted-saint.html.

4.   "Mary Karr Names Names," *The Fix*, May 22, 2013. http://www.thefix .com/content/mary-karr-liars-sober91684?page=all.

5.   This was originally stated on my blog at: http://www.patheos.com/ blogs/evetushnet/2012/10/to-come-first-for-someone.html.

6.   Matthew Franklin Jones (using the pseudonym Jordan), *Gay Subtlety*, "Wanted for Possession," June 7, 2012. http://gaysubtlety.wordpress .com/2012/06/07/wanted-for-possession/.

7.   Wesley Hill, *Washed and Waiting: Reflections on Christian Faithfulness and Homosexuality* (Grand Rapids, MI: Zondervan, 2010), 119.

8.   Ibid., 92.

Appendix 1

1.   Congregation for the Doctrine of the Faith, "Letter to the Bishops of the Catholic Church on the Pastoral Care of Homosexual Persons," October 1, 1986. Available at http://www.vatican.va/roman_curia/congregations/cfaith/ documents/rc_con_cfaith_doc_19861001_homosexual-persons_en.html.

2.   United States Conference of Catholic Bishops, "Always Our Children: A Pastoral Message to Parents of Homosexual Children and Suggestions for Pastoral Ministers," September 10, 1997.

Appendix 2

1.   Heather Moore, "Principal Forces High School Boys to Hold Hands as Punishment for Fight," CBS5 – KPHO, November 30, 2012. http://www.kpho .com/story/20224198/principal-forces-high-school-boys-to-hold-hands-as-punishment-for-fight.

Appendix 3

1.   Brent Bailey, *Odd Man Out*, "Safe People," October 9, 2012. http://odd-manout.net/post/33230777647/safe-people.

Eve Tushnet lives in Washington, DC, where she was raised some-where between atheism and Reform Judaism. She cofounded her high school's gay/straight alliance and entered the Catholic Church in 1998, during her sophomore year at Yale University. She is a freelance writer and in 2010, she was profiled in the *New York Times* "Beliefs" column.

Tushnet blogs regularly at *The American Conservative* and *Patheos*. Her work has been published by *The Atlantic, Weekly Standard, Commonweal,* and *First Things,* and she has written for the *Washington Post's* "On Faith" blog and the *New York Times* "Room for Debate." She has spoken on being gay and Catholic at Carnegie-Mellon University, Georgetown University, Princeton University, and Fordham, among others. She has also addressed a group of campus ministers in the Diocese of Pittsburgh and spoken with Interfaith Voices, a syndicated public radio show. Tushnet contributed an essay on gay Catholic life to the 2008 anthology *Faith at the Edge,* and has essays forthcoming in books from Fordham University Press and the University of Notre Dame Press.